Montaigne

Past Masters

AQUINAS Anthony Kenny
FRANCIS BACON Anthony Quinton
BURKE C. B. Macpherson
CONFUCIUS Raymond Dawson
DANTE George Holmes
ENGELS Terrell Carver
GALILEO Stillman Drake

HOMER Jasper Griffin
HUME A. J. Ayer
JESUS Humphrey Carpenter
MACHIAVELLI Quentin Skinner
MARX Peter Singer
MONTAIGNE Peter Burke
PASCAL Alban Krailsheimer

Forthcoming

ARISTOTLE Jonathan Barnes
AUGUSTINE Henry Chadwick
BACH Denis Arnold
BAYLE Elisabeth Labrousse
BERGSON Leszek Kolakowski
BERKELEY J. O. Urmson
THE BUDDHA Michael Carrithers
JOSEPH BUTLER R. G. Frey
CARLYLE A. L. Le Quesne
CERVANTES P. E. Russell
CHAUCER George Kane
CLAUSEWITZ Michael Howard
COBBETT Raymond Williams
COLERIDGE Richard Holmes
COPERNICUS Owen Gingerich
DARWIN Jonathan Howard
DIDEROT Peter France
ERASMUS James McConica
GIBBON J. W. Burrow
GODWIN Alan Ryan
GOETHE T. J. Reed
HEGEL Peter Singer

HERZEN Aileen Kelly
JEFFERSON Jack P. Greene
JOHNSON Pat Rogers
LAMARCK L. J. Jordanova
LINNAEUS W. T. Stearn
LOCKE John Dunn
MENDEL Vitezslav Orel
MILL William Thomas
THOMAS MORE Anthony Kenny
MORRIS Peter Stansky
MUHAMMAD Michael Cook
NEWMAN Owen Chadwick
NEWTON P. M. Rattansi
PETRARCH Nicholas Mann
PLATO R. M. Hare
RUSKIN George P. Landow
ST PAUL Tom Mills
SHAKESPEARE Germaine Greer
ADAM SMITH A. W. Coats
SOCRATES Bernard Williams
TOLSTOY Henry Gifford

and others

Peter Burke

MONTAIGNE

Oxford   Melbourne   Toronto

OXFORD UNIVERSITY PRESS

1981

Oxford University Press, Walton Street, Oxford OX2 6DP

London Glasgow New York Toronto
Delhi Bombay Calcutta Madras Karachi
Kuala Lumpur Singapore Hong Kong Tokyo
Nairobi Dar es Salaam Cape Town
Melbourne Wellington

and associate companies in
Beirut Berlin Ibadan Mexico City

British Library Cataloguing in Publication Data
Burke, Peter
  Montaigne. – (Past masters)
  1. Montaigne, Michel de – Criticism and
  interpretation
  I. Title   II. Series
  844'.3   PQ1643
  ISBN 0-19-287523-X

Printed in Great Britain by
Cox & Wyman Ltd, Reading

Preface

As an intellectual historian let loose in a field traditionally grazed by students of literature, I am particularly grateful to Dorothy Coleman, Margaret McGowan, and Ruth Morse for their comments on earlier drafts. I should also like to thank Henry Hardy, Quentin Skinner and Keith Thomas for their criticisms and suggestions, and Riccardo Steiner for drawing my attention to Freud's interest in Montaigne, and Montaigne's fortune in Italy.

All translations of Montaigne are my own. References in parentheses to quotations from the *Essays* are to book and chapter respectively.

P. B.

Contents

For Sue

1 Montaigne in his time

Like Shakespeare, Montaigne is, in a sense, our contemporary. Few writers of the sixteenth century are easier to read today, or speak to us as directly and immediately as he does. It is difficult not to like Montaigne, and almost equally difficult not to treat him as one of ourselves. He was a critic of intellectual authority before the Enlightenment, a cool observer of human sexuality before psychoanalysis, and a dispassionate student of other cultures before the rise of social anthropology. It is easy to see him as a modern born out of his time.

However, Montaigne is not as modern as he looks. His interest in autobiographical details may seem reminiscent of the Romantics, but his self-analysis was undertaken for different reasons. Although he was a sceptic, he was not an agnostic in the modern sense. To call him a 'liberal' or a 'conservative' in the sense in which we use these terms today is equally to misunderstand his position. Montaigne shared interests, attitudes, values and assumptions – in other words, a whole mentality – with his contemporaries, more particularly with those who belonged to the same social group and the same generation as he did. Other Frenchmen of his time, besides Montaigne, had doubts about the power of human reason to reach the truth, condemned both parties in the civil wars, and published short discourses on various subjects. Indeed, some of the topics on which he chose to write were commonplaces of the day; it is what he made of them that distinguishes him from his contemporaries. He was a true, if not a typical, sixteenth-century man. This does not mean that he has nothing to say to us. He challenges our assumptions as he did those of his own generation.

Montaigne was not a systematic thinker. Indeed, he presented his ideas in a deliberately unsystematic way. As a result there are serious dangers awaiting anyone who attempts to give a systematic account of his thought. Such an account naturally takes the form of quotations with a commentary elucidating

them. These quotations have to be taken out of their original
context. To treat Montaigne's work in this way is peculiarly
dangerous because he relied on context to an unusual extent. He
liked to be ambiguous and ironic. He liked to quote other
writers, but also to play the quotations off against their new
context to give them another meaning. One of the pleasures in
reading Montaigne is that one constantly finds fresh possible
meanings in his writings; the difficulty is to decide whether a
given meaning was intended or not. There is no infallible way
of doing this, and all firm assertions about Montaigne's beliefs
should be treated with scepticism. However, we will have no
chance at all of understanding him if we do not replace him in
his social and cultural milieu.

Michel Eyquem de Montaigne was born in 1533. He belonged
to what might be called the 'generation of the 1530s'. Genera-
tions cannot be calculated exactly; they are definable in social
and cultural terms as much as by dates of birth, held together as
they are by a sense of community deriving from common experience. The generation of the 1530s, in France, was the first
group which had no memory of the world before the Reforma-
tion. This group includes the lawyer-historian Etienne Pasquier
(born in 1529), an acquaintance of Montaigne and a great admirer of the *Essays*; Montaigne's best friend, Etienne de La
Boétie (1530); Jean Bodin (*c.*1530), the leading intellectual of
later sixteenth-century France, a man whom Montaigne greatly
esteemed, although he rejected his views on witchcraft; the
scholar-printer Henri Etienne (1531), and the gentleman-
soldier François de La Noue (1531), both Calvinists (Calvin
himself, born in 1509, belonged to an older generation). It is
perhaps worth stretching this notion of a 'generation of the
1530s' to include at one end Pierre Charron (1540), who was an
intellectual disciple of Montaigne's, and at the other Pierre Ronsard (1524) and Marc-Antoine Muret (1526), who was one of
Montaigne's teachers.

Whether they opted for Catholicism, Calvinism, or something more unusual (Bodin is believed to have turned Jew), this
generation had to come to terms with an unprecedented division
of opinion over issues generally considered to be absolutely

fundamental. Montaigne's experience of religious divisions within his family (his sister Jeanne became a Calvinist, and so, for a time, did his brother Thomas, while his father remained a staunch Catholic), was far from untypical. A preoccupation with the problem of religious diversity was characteristic of the time, although Montaigne's attitude was very much his own.

As important as a knowledge of his generation for understanding the ideas of Montaigne is a knowledge of the social group to which he belonged. He was the eldest son and heir of a Gascon gentleman, Pierre Eyquem. However, his mother, Antoinette de Loupes, was of Spanish origin, and probably Jewish (though her family had lived in France for centuries), and his father's nobility was of relatively recent vintage. 'Vintage' is the appropriate word, for there were wine merchants in the recent past of his family, which lived and owned land not far from Bordeaux. One might say that Château d'Yquem flowed in Montaigne's veins, but it should be added that he was not proud of his origins. A fourth-generation nobleman, he was the first of his line to drop the surname 'Eyquem' and call himself by the name of the estate he inherited, Montaigne. He described his family, not quite accurately, as famous for 'valour' (*preud'homie*, the characteristic virtue of the medieval knight). He liked to refer to himself as a soldier, the basic role of the traditional nobility, although his principal occupation, between university and early retirement, was in fact that of magistrate (*conseiller*) in the court (*parlement*) of Bordeaux, a post he held from 1557 to 1570. In practice he was closer to the new legal nobility (*noblesse de robe*), into which he married, than to the older military nobility (*noblesse d'épée*).

These military nobles were traditionally no lovers of learning, and Montaigne's frequent protestations that he was not a scholar should not be understood in terms of personal modesty, true or false, but as commonplaces expected from the social group with which he identified. His reflections on the education of children (1.26) are explicitly concerned with the training of a gentleman, and they emphasise the need to avoid what he calls pedantry. The ideal is that of the amateur, the dilettante. In similar fashion Montaigne liked to give the impression that he did not study, but simply browsed through his books from time to time 'without order, without method'; that he did not polish what he wrote, but simply put down whatever came into his head; and that his aim in writing, as he declared in the preface to the *Essays*, was purely 'domestic and private', for the sake of his family and friends, not for the general public. This was the only form of writing of which a French gentleman of the time had no need to be ashamed.

The extent to which Montaigne held the views contemporaries expected from a member of the French nobility should not be exaggerated. If he had been typical, we would not remember him at all. To come a little closer to appreciating the blend of the distinctive and the conventional in his attitudes, it may be useful to look at one of the major decisions in his life: retirement. In 1570 he sold his post as magistrate – the sale of such offices was normal at the time – and retired to the country estate which he had inherited on his father's death two years earlier. He withdrew to his library on the third floor of a round tower, a room which he decorated with inscriptions in Greek and Latin. There, he told his readers, he spent 'most of his days, and most hours of the day' (3.3).

Why did he retire? The most obvious explanation is political. Montaigne later described his estate as 'my retreat, to rest myself from wars' (2.15). By 1570 the civil wars had been raging for eight years. Michel de L'Hôpital, chancellor of France, who had tried in vain to prevent Catholics and Protestants from killing one another, had given up the struggle in 1568 and retired to his estate at Vignay. In any case, Montaigne was thirty-seven in 1570. A few years later, he would describe himself as 'well on the way to old age, having long since crossed the threshold of forty' (2.17). It seems that he thought of his retirement more or less like a modern sixty-year-old. This idea was not a morbid peculiarity of his. In the sixteenth century, it was perfectly normal for people to consider themselves old at forty. What we perceive as the mid-life crisis, leading to awareness that the future is circumscribed and to what one psychiatrist calls 'constructive resignation' was perceived in the sixteenth century as the end-of-life crisis, and often with good reason. Although

Montaigne had in reality twenty-two years to go in 1570, his great friend Etienne de La Boétie had died in 1563 at the age of thirty-two, and the poet Joachim du Bellay had died in 1560 at the age of thirty-seven. That Montaigne retired to prepare for death is suggested by the fact that a major theme of his essays is what contemporaries called the 'art of dying well'.

Montaigne saw his retirement as the beginning of his end, although it turned out to be no more than the end of his beginning. He was to leave his tower to visit Germany, Switzerland and Italy in 1580–1, and to serve two terms as mayor of Bordeaux on his return (1581–5). In 1588, he was involved in the negotiations between the king, Henri III, and the Protestant leader, Henri de Navarre (later Henri IV). In the intervals between these activities, he wrote the *Essays*.

As for the decision to bury himself in the country, which may seem odd in a man who disliked cultivating his garden, let alone hunting and estate management, this too was conventional. For the élites of Renaissance Europe, as of ancient Rome, the countryside was associated with learned leisure (*otium*), just as the city was associated with business, in the sense of political affairs (*negotium*). An inscription in Montaigne's library, dating from 1571, dedicates it to liberty, tranquillity and leisure, and describes its owner as 'quite weary of service to the court and of public office'. Montaigne thus situated himself in a long and distinguished tradition of the rejection of public life, more particularly life at the courts of princes, a rejection expressed by many ancient and modern writers, such as Horace (one of his favourite authors), the Spanish bishop Antonio de Guevara, whose *Contempt for the Court and Praise of the Country* (1539) was also well known to him, and the *Pleasures of Rural Life* of the Gascon gentleman Guy du Faur de Pibrac (1529–84), whom he admired as 'a noble spirit'.

Montaigne's retirement was an escape from society, but it was a mode of escape which was structured by society and reflected the contemporary ideal of studious leisure. The former chancellor, Michel de L'Hôpital, spent his retirement composing Latin verse, where his modern equivalent would settle down to write his memoirs. L'Hôpital conformed to the ideal of the

Renaissance humanist. There is a good case for regarding Montaigne too as a humanist.

2 Montaigne's humanism

Since Jacob Burckhardt's famous study of *The Civilisation of the Renaissance in Italy* (1860), the concept 'humanism' has been popular with historians, but they have not all used it in the same way. Some of them use the term in a fairly vague sense to mean concern with the dignity of man, and contrast a man-centred Renaissance – at times rather too simply – with a God-centred Middle Ages. Other historians prefer to use the term 'humanist' in the way in which contemporaries employed the term *umanista*, which was part of student slang in Italian universities about 1500. A humanist in this sense was a professional teacher of the 'humanities' (*studia humanitatis*), that is, of history, ethics, poetry and rhetoric. These four subjects were considered particularly 'humane' by Cicero and other Roman intellectuals, and again at the Renaissance, because it was believed that man's essential characteristics were his ability to speak and to tell right from wrong.

Renaissance humanists in this sense of the term stood out from their academic colleagues by their rejection of the 'schoolmen' (*scholastici*), that is, medieval philosophers such as Thomas Aquinas, Duns Scotus and William of Ockham, and their master Aristotle. The humanists disliked both the language of scholastic philosophy, which was unclassical (and therefore, in their eyes, barbarous), and its concentration on logic, which they considered arid and lacking in relevance compared to the study of ethics. They rejected the culture of what they were the first to call the 'Middle Ages' in favour of classical models for both language and behaviour. Cicero showed them how to write; Socrates, Cato and Scipio showed them how to die and how to live.

The humanist movement, which flourished in the fifteenth and sixteenth centuries, lasted too long and involved too many people to be uniform or unchanging. Some humanists admired Julius Caesar; others preferred Brutus, his assassin. Some humanists, now often described as 'civic', thought the life of action superior to that of contemplation. They would have considered that Montaigne was fulfilling himself administering Bordeaux rather than sitting in his tower. Other humanists believed exactly the opposite. Some concerned themselves with rhetoric, others with philosophy, and there were many conflicts between the two groups. Some humanists followed Plato, others Aristotle (though unlike the schoolmen, they read him in Greek), and yet others the stoics, especially the Roman philosopher Seneca (4 BC–AD 65), and the ideal of 'constancy' expressed in his *Letters to Lucilius*. The constant man, according to Seneca, travels light through life. He knows how to limit his desires and for this reason he stands as unmoved by the buffetings of inconstant fortune as an oak tree in the wind. This is a good philosophy for bad times, and it is scarcely surprising that it seemed particularly attractive to European intellectuals during the religious wars of the later sixteenth century. In France, Montaigne's brother-in-law Pressac (1574) and the Calvinist nobleman Mornay (1576) both translated Seneca's letters. In the Netherlands, which also suffered what he called 'the tempest of civil wars', the great scholar Justus Lipsius, an admirer of Montaigne, edited Seneca and wrote his own treatise *On Constancy* (1585). Around 1590 the French lawyer Guillaume Du Vair wrote a book on the same subject, which became quite popular.

Diverse as they were (or became), the humanists shared an admiration for classical antiquity, a belief that the wisdom of the ancients could be reconciled with Christianity, and a central concern with man. Like Socrates, they thought self-knowledge the important thing, not the knowledge of nature. They liked to quote a saying of the Greek philosopher Protagoras (*c.* 485–*c.* 415 BC), the somewhat cryptic remark that 'of all things the measure is man, of the things that are, that they are, and of the things that are not, that they are not'.

Montaigne was no humanist in the strict professional sense, like (say) Adrien Turnèbe, professor of Greek at the Collège royal in Paris, who, he wrote, 'knew everything', and was the greatest scholar for 'a thousand years'. However, he did share humanist interests and attitudes. Although he may have had little Greek, his Latin was excellent. Thanks to his father's taste for educational experiment, Latin was literally Montaigne's first language. Nothing else was spoken to him, he tells us, until he was six (1.26). As a result, he was reading Ovid for fun at an age when other boys were reading romances of chivalry – the westerns of the sixteenth century – if they were reading at all. Montaigne went on to receive a thorough humanist education at the newly-founded Collège de Guyenne at Bordeaux, which, besides being conveniently near at hand, was one of the best schools of the new kind to be found in Europe at that time. He was taught by humanists who later became famous, notably Marc-Antoine Muret and the Scotsman George Buchanan, and acted in the Latin tragedies they composed. It is likely, though it cannot be proved, that he went on to study with Turnèbe and others at the University of Paris.

This education left its mark. We have already seen how Montaigne regarded his retirement from public life in classical or humanist terms. About five years later, he had fifty-seven maxims painted on the beams of his library, just as the humanist Marsilio Ficino had had maxims painted on the study walls of his villa at Careggi in Tuscany. Twenty-five of Montaigne's maxims were quotations from Greek, and thirty-two from Latin, including one from the Roman playwright Terence (*c.* 195–159 BC) which might stand as a motto for humanism in its wide sense: 'I am a man, I consider nothing human to be alien to me' (*Homo sum, humani a me nihil alienum puto*).

It is a rare essay which is not stuffed with Latin quotations (1,264 of them altogether). Montaigne often got his quotations at second hand, as he frankly admits, but it is clear from his references and borrowings that his favourite authors were all ancients. Nine Romans and two Greeks are quoted more often than any post-classical writers. His favourites are, in ascending order of importance, Ovid, Tacitus, Herodotus, Caesar, Virgil, Diogenes Laertius (author of *Lives of the Philosophers*, and used for what the philosophers said rather than for what he said about them), Horace, Lucretius, Cicero, Seneca and Plutarch. Montaigne shared the admiration of his contemporaries for Seneca, and especially for the *Letters to Lucilius*. Some of the earliest essays are little more than mosaics of quotations from the Roman philosopher (Montaigne himself speaks of 'inlay'), and the informal, un-Ciceronian prose of the *Essays* also owes a great deal to Seneca. As for the works of Plutarch (*c.* 46–*c.* 127 AD), Montaigne studied them carefully in the new French translation by the bishop Jacques Amyot, and he refers to them or borrows from the moral discourses and the lives of famous Greeks and Romans nearly four hundred times in the course of his *Essays*. Like Henri IV, he might have called Plutarch his 'conscience'. His favourite poets, like his favourite philosophers, were classical; not only Ovid and Horace, but Catullus, Martial and Juvenal.

Montaigne's heroes are all ancients as well. The discussion of 'the most excellent men' (2.36) centres on Homer, Alexander the Great, and, in the highest place of all, the Theban general Epaminondas (died 362 BC). Later, it was Socrates who became Montaigne's hero, 'this incomparable man', 'the wisest man who ever existed', 'the most perfect who ever came to my knowledge'. Montaigne thought his own age mediocre compared to the glories of antiquity, and the ancients were his point of reference for judging the present, just as they were for the humanists.

Like the humanists, Montaigne had little time for the schoolmen, or for 'the god of scholastic learning' Aristotle, at least not for his *Logic* or *Metaphysics*. When, relatively late, Montaigne discovered the *Ethics* and the *Politics*, he appreciated them much more, and in this respect too he was a man of his time. Like Socrates, Cicero, and the humanists, he believed that the proper study of mankind is man: the human condition, not the physical universe. The first thing a child had to learn, he wrote, was 'to know himself, to know how to die well and how to live well' (1.26). Montaigne was not ignorant of the physical sciences. He was aware of the heliocentric theory of Copernicus as he was aware of 'the atoms of Epicurus, or the fullness and emptiness of Leucippus and Democritus, or the water of Thales' (2.12), but these abstract ideas did not awaken his curiosity. He did not care whether Copernicus or Ptolemy was right, whether the sun revolved around the earth or the earth around the sun. Montaigne was rather more interested in contemporary technology, in ingenious machines, as is revealed by the journal of his foreign travels, with its careful descriptions of the automatic gates at Nuremberg and the 'miraculous' grotto at Pratolino in Tuscany, where water power caused statues to move and music to play. However, when he reached Rome, his enthusiasms were those of any humanist. He went to the Vatican Library and admired the manuscripts of his favourite authors, Plutarch and Seneca, and he spent days in the study of the physical remains of the classical city. He praised ancient and modern works of art, but had little to say about them.

Montaigne has sometimes been presented as a critic of humanism, as part of a 'Counter-Renaissance'. It is not altogether clear what he thought of the major humanists of his century. He owed a good deal to Erasmus, but rarely referred to him, perhaps because the Church had come to associate Erasmus with Luther. He disliked pedantry and made fun in a somewhat Erasmian way of the scholar burning the midnight oil: 'do you think he is searching in his books for a way to become better, happier or wiser? Nothing of the kind. He will teach posterity the metre of Plautus's verses, and the correct spelling of a Latin word, or he will die in the attempt' (1.39). On occasion, like Erasmus again, Montaigne criticised the stoic ideal of the constant man, 'an immobile and impassive Colossus', as unnatural, perhaps inhuman (1.44). If the humanists were uncritical believers in the value of classical philology, rhetoric, the dignity of man and the power of human reason, then there can be no doubt of Montaigne's detachment from their attitudes; but, as the example of Erasmus indicates, this is to simplify the movement unduly. There were humanists who criticised rhetoric or wrote against the stoics just as there were ancient writers who did so, Plutarch for example, showing himself once again a man after Montaigne's heart.

As for the dignity of man, it would be a mistake to draw too strong a contrast between Pico della Mirandola's famous *Oration on the Dignity of Man* and Montaigne's no less famous puncturing of human pretensions in his 'Apologia for Raymond Sebond' (2.12). It is true that Montaigne is turning Pico on his head, and arguing for the littleness of man, 'this miserable and wretched creature, who is not even master of himself . . . and yet dares to call himself lord and emperor of this universe.' The disagreements of the philosophers, the wisdom of animals – like the dog who 'deduces' with his nose which way his master has gone – the unreliability of sense-data, and many other arguments are pressed into service to combat human vanity and presumption, and especially the idea that it is the use of reason which distinguishes man from beast. Montaigne brings out the stock humanist quotation from Protagoras only to pour scorn on it: 'Truly Protagoras told us a tall story, making man the measure of all things, when he had never taken his own' (2.12).

However, the humanists were not unaware of human weaknesses. Their rhetorical set-pieces on the dignity of man often went with companion-pieces on his misery, laying out the arguments for and against, as the French writer Pierre Boaystuau did in his *Theatre of the World* (1559), a book which was in Montaigne's library. Pico was putting a case for one side, and Montaigne for the other. The apologia is a set-piece, very different in tone from the other essays. Despite his claim to distrust rhetoric, what Montaigne has given us here is a brilliant oration on man's misery. It was not the whole story, and he knew it. Elsewhere he suggested that 'There is nothing so fine and so legitimate as to play the man well and properly, nor is there any science so difficult as to know how to live this life well and according to nature; and of all our infirmities the most serious is to despise our being' (3.13).

Montaigne was not a 'typical' humanist – if there is such a thing. He was too much the individualist for that. He was certainly no neoplatonist, as many humanists were. He thought Plato's dialogues were boring, and no doubt enjoyed what he called his 'sacrilegious boldness' in saying so in public. He considered it better to know one's own language well, and perhaps the language of a neighbouring country into the bargain, than to know Latin and Greek; in this respect he had certainly reacted against the education given him by his father. He did not think that the ancients were authoritative. Unlike most of his contemporaries, Montaigne did not believe in authorities (apart from the Church). As we have seen, he thought much classical learning useless pedantry. He declared that he would rather understand himself than understand Cicero. He had little faith in human reason. An eccentric humanist, without doubt. If, after all these qualifications, the term still seems appropriate, it is on account of Montaigne's constant use of classical antiquity as a point of reference, and of his admiration for certain individual ancients, such as Socrates and Plutarch.

It is not difficult to see why Montaigne admired Socrates, whose awareness of his own ignorance, insistence on self-knowledge, contempt for the professional sophists, informality and irony all remind us of Montaigne himself. In the case of Plutarch too there was a marriage of true minds. Plutarch was a philosopher, but also a practical man, a patrician who had held public office both at Delphi and in his native Chaeronea. His concern with how to live is revealed in his parallel lives of famous Greeks and Romans as well as in his ethical discourses, which were translated into French in 1572, just in time for Montaigne to make use of them. He has one discourse on the rationality of animals, from which Montaigne borrowed for his apologia, another on the affection of parents for their children, echoed by Montaigne's essay on that subject, and others, from which Montaigne also learned a good deal, on the decline of oracles and on 'superstition'. More generally, the self-revelation, the humour and the colloquial tone of these discourses remind us of Montaigne, as do the frequent digressions and the still more frequent quotations (Erasmus referred to Plutarch's 'mosaic'). It is clear that Plutarch, even more than Seneca, helped Montaigne to find his own voice.

This was, of course, the great function of the classical writers for Renaissance humanists. They were 'past masters'. To call Montaigne a humanist is to place him in a cultural tradition without which it would be difficult to understand the *Essays*. But we have seen that Montaigne was a humanist of a particular generation, which faced intellectual problems rather different from those of its predecessors. One of the most serious of these problems is the subject of the next chapter.

3 Montaigne's scepticism

Que sais-je? What do I know? is the phrase which posterity has associated most closely with Montaigne. With reason: it was quite literally his motto, which appeared on one side of a medal which he had struck, in true Renaissance style, in the middle of the 1570s. On the other side there was a pair of scales in suspense, making the same point in visual terms. On the beams of Montaigne's study was painted 'all that is certain is that nothing is certain', and 'I suspend judgement'. The last phrase was one of eight quotations, all to the same effect, from the late classical philosopher Sextus Empiricus.

Sextus, who flourished around AD 200, was the author of the *Hypotyposes* or 'outlines' of scepticism, an introduction to the subject which survived when the writings of the philosophers on whom it was based (such as Pyrrho of Elis, after whom scepticism is sometimes called 'pyrrhonism'), were lost. He defines the basic principle of scepticism as that of 'opposing to every proposition an equal proposition', and of suspending judgement between the two, on the grounds that we do not and cannot know which is correct. Sextus argues the case for scepticism on a number of grounds. One is the unreliability of our senses. 'The same impressions are not produced by the same objects', for, to take a commonly repeated example, 'sufferers from jaundice declare that objects which seem to us white are yellow.' Again, our reaction to a particular kind of occurrence, such as the appearance of a meteor in the sky, varies with its frequency or rarity; so the same occurrence seems normal at one time and amazing at another. Another argument for scepticism is the diversity of human judgements and customs. 'Indians enjoy some things, our people other things . . . Some of the Ethiopians tattoo their children, but we do not . . . and whereas the Indians have intercourse with their woman in public, most other races regard this as shameful.' It seems impossible to avoid relativism, that is the conclusion that all customs are as good as one another.

Once again, judgement is suspended. Of course one cannot live in a state of permanent suspense and Sextus recommends in practice that we live 'a life conformable with the customs of our country and its laws and institutions'. What he opposes is dogmatism, the confidence that our own customs and attitudes are right and those of others wrong. Sextus even criticised the Greek philosopher Protagoras, as Montaigne was to do, for making man 'the measure of all things', in other words for ethnocentrism at the level of the whole human race.

Sextus's position is an elaboration of that of Socrates, who was reported as saying that he knew nothing except that he knew nothing. Another classic statement of the sceptical position comes in Cicero's *Academica* (written about 45 BC), a dialogue which discusses the views of Arcesilas, a philosopher of the 'New Academy' who went even further than Socrates and declared that we could not even be certain that nothing was certain; a reflexive, self-critical scepticism.

In the Middle Ages, Sextus's book was lost and little interest seems to have been taken in epistemological debates of this kind until the fourteenth century, when the English philosopher William of Ockham (*c.* 1300–49) argued that it was impossible to prove by human reason that God is infinite or omniscient or even that there is one God rather than many. Unlike the classical sceptics, he did not doubt our knowledge of this world; what Ockham did was to separate the realms of faith and reason, as the philosophers of the Muslim world had been doing. In the fifteenth century, Nicholas of Cusa's *On Learned Ignorance* – a book known to Montaigne – explored the converse of Ockham, in other words the possibility of knowing God by non-rational means.

Ockham's ideas were well known in the sixteenth century; they were taught in many universities. It is likely that they made ancient scepticism somewhat easier to accept when it was rediscovered, that they diminished intellectual resistance to Pyrrhonist ideas. It is also likely that the ancient sceptics were viewed through Ockhamist spectacles. A synthesis of the two intellectual traditions was sketched by Erasmus. In his *Praise of Folly* (1509) – another book in Montaigne's library – Erasmus exploited to the full the paradoxical possibilities of a mock-oration in praise of folly delivered by Folly herself, used scepticism to undermine what he regarded as the dogmatism of the scholastic philosophers, and ended in the manner of Nicholas of Cusa (and St Paul) by presenting Christianity as a form of folly which is superior to wisdom. Erasmus thus joined together themes from the classical and Christian traditions.

So did Gianfrancesco Pico della Mirandola, the nephew of the Pico who had written on the dignity of man. His *Examination of the Vanity of the Doctrine of the Pagans* (1520) uses Sextus (although it was not yet in print), to attack both classical philosophy and divination, chiromancy, geomancy and so on, which was taken seriously by many of the educated as well as by ordinary people at this time. For Gianfrancesco Pico, the true sources of knowledge are prophecy and revelation. More like Erasmus's book in its air of wilful paradox, the German humanist Agrippa of Nettesheim's *On the Uncertainty and Vanity of the Sciences* (1526) takes each branch of knowledge in turn and demolishes its claims to truth. Sceptical of rational roads to knowledge and power, Agrippa seems to have believed in the efficacy of non-rational roads to the same destination, for he was a practising magician. His work too was known to Montaigne.

Around the middle of the sixteenth century, when Montaigne was a student, a group of Paris intellectuals was taking considerable interest in these epistemological issues. Petrus Ramus, one of the most controversial figures at the university, was attacking Aristotle and being denounced by the Aristotelians as a sceptic. A young lawyer, Guy de Bruès, published *Dialogues against the New Academics* (1558), a creative imitation of Cicero's *Academica* which discussed not only the problem of knowledge but also that of legal relativism. In the 1560s, two Latin versions of Sextus's *Hypotyposes* were published in Paris. In 1576, the philosopher Francisco Sanchez wrote a critique of Aristotle and of medieval logicians entitled 'Nothing is known' (*Quod Nihil Scitur*). Sanchez was an old boy of Montaigne's school, the Collège de Guyenne. Whether Montaigne knew his work or not – and it was not published till 1581, a year after the *Essays* – it is another illustration of the appeal of scepticism to Montaigne's generation.

The point of this account of the development of scepticism in western culture is to stop anyone thinking that Montaigne went into his tower to go through what has been called his 'sceptical crisis' in isolation. He had retired from public life, but he was not isolated intellectually. He read Sextus, Cicero, Erasmus, Agrippa, de Bruès and others. In France in his day, the problem of knowledge might even be described as topical.

The problem certainly fascinated Montaigne. From the first essays to the last, he stresses the variety and consequently the unreliability of human opinions. 'No two men ever had the same opinion of the same thing' (3.13). He pours scorn alike on the predictions of the palm-readers and the diagnoses of the physicians, noting the disagreements among the practitioners of both arts over the ways in which the 'signs' are to be read. Individually, Montaigne's sceptical ideas are reminiscent of his predecessors, but the combination is his own. Like Erasmus, he exploits his opportunities for irony to the full. Like Gianfrancesco Pico, he makes a point of attacking diviners; unlike him, Montaigne is also critical of prophecy. Like Sextus, and more recently, de Bruès, he makes the diversity of customs and laws one of the most important arguments for scepticism. Like Sanchez, he also stresses changes in opinions over time, and interprets change as evidence of unreliability.

How seriously did Montaigne takes his sceptical arguments? The answer is far from clear. We cannot be sure whether he passed through a personal 'crisis' or just employed doubt as a rhetorical device, though the recurrence of sceptical themes in the essays makes the first conclusion appear the more likely. It is difficult, in any case, to consider these epistemological questions for any length of time without a strong and unpleasant sensation of intellectual vertigo. Again, we cannot be sure whether Montaigne was opposed to reason or simply to dogmatism. He seems to use the term *raison* in a variety of ways, to accept *raison universelle* (the principles underlying nature and culture), while rejecting *raison humaine*; but here too it is necessary to distinguish a hostile attitude to theorising from a favourable attitude to what might be called 'practical reason'. He praised the sceptics because 'they use their reason to enquire and debate', though not to choose (2.12). This was precisely the procedure he followed in his essays. In any case, whether he was wilfully or unconsciously inconsistent, his scepticism did not prevent Montaigne from making all sorts of grand general statements like 'every movement reveals us', or 'the world is in a state of incessant change'.

The question of Montaigne's doubts and how far he went with them is obviously a crucial one to any interpretation of his thought. On our answer to this question, our interpretation of his religious or political attitudes necessarily depends. The reader is invited to bear this point in mind and also to suspend judgement – at least for a time – while reading the chapters which follow.

4 Montaigne's religion

It is scarcely surprising that Montaigne found scepticism attractive, for his generation, the generation of the 1530s, had to face a problem which was new, acute and urgent. Which form of Christianity should they choose – Catholic or Protestant? What is more, the theologians of each party had been undermining the foundations of the beliefs of the other. The Protestants had questioned the authority of tradition, and the Catholics had in turn cast doubt on the authority of the Bible. The results of this 'shaking of the foundations' were serious, according to Montaigne, and such as neither party intended:

for the vulgar ... once they are emboldened to criticise and condemn the opinions they had previously held sacred (like matters of salvation), and once they see that some articles of their religion have been called into question, will soon come to regard their other beliefs as equally uncertain and to accept nothing at all on authority. (2.12)

In this crisis, Montaigne was requested to translate the *Natural Theology* (or *Book of Creatures*) of the fifteenth-century Catalan writer Raymond Sebond. The translation, which was published in 1569, was Montaigne's literary apprenticeship. The *Natural Theology*, a stout volume of nearly a thousand pages, describes Nature as a book, given us, like the Bible, to reveal the existence of God. Nature is described as a hierarchical society with man at the top, the most noble and perfect part of God's creation. Sebond's book is a 'natural theology' in the sense of a theology based on reason, without the aid of faith or revelation. It echoes the ideas of contemporary humanists concerning the dignity of man.

Whether or not it was of use to his father, who commissioned the translation, the *Natural Theology* does not seem to have done very much for Montaigne, who was, as we have seen, plagued by doubts in the middle 1570s. It was at this time that he wrote one of the most famous of his essays, the 'Apologia for Raymond

Sebond' (2.12). Couched as a defence of Sebond's natural theology, it is in fact precisely the opposite, a sceptic's demolition of the pretensions of human reason. It argues that man is presumptuous to think himself the most noble creature in the universe, since the animals have as much practical reason as we do, while our theoretical reason is unreliable, and its conclusions uncertain.

To a twentieth-century reader, Montaigne may well appear to be an agnostic; but appearances are misleading. His scepticism is very different from modern agnosticism. The term 'agnosticism' was coined in 1869 by the scientist T. H. Huxley to describe the belief that we cannot know God or any alleged reality beyond phenomena. That is, Huxley had his doubts about the 'supernatural', but trusted phenomena and human reason. Montaigne's view was more or less the opposite. He not trust phenomena (more exactly, he did not trust human perceptions of phenomena), and he did not trust human reason, but he seems to have had faith in faith. The apologia concludes that faith alone can embrace the mysteries of Christianity and that man can only raise himself above humanity if God lends him a helping hand.

This view is known nowadays as 'fideism', a term coined in the nineteenth century to describe a rejection of natural theology on somewhat different grounds. Montaigne's drily sceptical obedience is distinct from Kierkegaard's more emotional leap of faith. It was not an unusual view for a sixteenth-century Christian to hold. There was a strong tradition of natural theology, exemplified by greater men than Sebond, such as Thomas Aquinas, who tried to demonstrate the existence of God by five separate arguments all based on human reason alone. This is what Montaigne was rejecting. However, there was also a strong anti-rational tradition within Christianity (or at least, anti-rational tendencies), running from St Paul (four quotations from whom were painted on Montaigne's ceiling), through St Augustine and William of Ockham (who declared it impossible to prove God's existence by 'natural reason'), to the sixteenth century. Luther, for example, was a fideist who mocked 'Lady Reason' for judging divine things by a human measure. Montaigne's father took Raymond Sebond as an antidote to Lutheranism, but Montaigne's apologia sounds more like Luther. However, there were Catholic fideists as well as Protestant ones. Gianfrancesco Pico della Mirandola, whose attack on pagan learning has been discussed already, was one of them. For a Catholic to express scepticism about the validity of natural theology was not unorthodox in the middle of the sixteenth century. Indeed, Sebond's prologue had been condemned by the Church in 1559 precisely because it claimed too much for reason.

The middle of the sixteenth century was a time when the Church was changing. The Council of Trent, which first met in the 1540s but issued its main decrees in 1562–3, was a watershed in the history of Catholicism because it defined orthodoxy on a number of questions which had previously been open, or at least half-open. This was the moment when justification by faith was declared heretical; when the Vulgate, the traditional Latin version of the Bible, was declared official, at the expense of both Greek and Hebrew texts and of translations into the vernacular; and that the much-criticised cult of saints and their relics was reaffirmed. Orthodoxy was reinforced more thoroughly than before, by means of the Inquisition and the Index of Prohibited Books. The result of these decrees was to divide Europe into two camps, Catholic and Protestant, where there had been a wider, vaguer spectrum of religious opinion.

Where exactly did Montaigne stand? He seems to have behaved like an orthodox Catholic of the period following the Council of Trent. On his visit to Rome, so his journal informs us, he listened with pleasure to the Lenten sermons, and he went, like any other pilgrim, to see the relics, like the Veronica in St Peter's and the heads of Saints Peter and Paul in St John Lateran. He also made a visit to the Holy House of Loreto, one of the most popular Catholic shrines of the day, and spent fifty *écus*, no mean sum, on images and candles. Whenever he wrote about the French religious wars, he called the Catholic party 'us'. He also expressed some sympathy for the new-style Catholicism associated with Trent. He had words of admiration for the austerities of San Carlo Borromeo, the ascetic, militant archbishop of Milan. He believed that there was 'much more danger than profit' in the translation of the Bible into the vernacular; who would be competent to check the accuracy of the translations into Basque or Breton? In any case, he wrote, the Bible 'is not for everyone to study'. In the same essay he went out of his way to declare his intention to write nothing contrary to the doctrines of 'the Catholic, Apostolic and Roman Church in which I was born and in which I shall die', adding that he submitted his ideas to 'the judgement of those to whom it belongs to direct not only my actions and my writings, but my thoughts as well' (1.56). Montaigne here gave his public assent to the Church's right to thought control, and to the attitude of mind recommended by St Ignatius in his *Spiritual Exercises* (1548): 'I will believe that the white object I see is black if that should be the decision of the hierarchical Church.' After all, sceptics knew that the senses could not be trusted.

However, Montaigne was no ordinary Catholic. No ordinary Catholic layman published his ideas on religious matters, still less such unusual ideas as Montaigne's were for their period. His ideas on miracles, for example. The conventional Catholic view was that miracles are suspensions of the law of nature, specially permitted by God. Montaigne's view was that 'miracles depend on our ignorance of nature, not on nature itself.' It is the strange event which is called miraculous, and ideas of what is strange are necessarily ethnocentric. 'The barbarians are no more strange to us, than we are to them' (1.23). Montaigne was echoing Cicero and Sextus Empiricus on the relativity of 'wonders', and the word he uses, *miracle*, was the ordinary word for 'wonder'. However, the circumstances of the day, not so long after the Church had reaffirmed the importance of miracle-working saints and relics, gave his remark a significance rather different from anything that Cicero or Sextus said. To make the same point in a different situation is to say something different. Montaigne's epigram is opaque, perhaps deliberately so. He seems to be saying that although miracles do occur, we cannot know, in any given instance, whether a miracle has occurred or not. The Church did claim to know, but Montaigne's 'we' may well refer to unaided human reason. On the other hand, it is possible that

Montaigne intended to make a much more radical suggestion, and that is that the very concept of a miracle (or any other wonder) is meaningless because it is ethnocentric. Montaigne's belief in the variety of nature inclined him not to take its 'laws' very seriously, and if there are no laws, there is nothing to suspend.

In similar fashion, Montaigne thought conventional Christian views of Providence should be dismissed as ethnocentric.

> If the frost nips the vines in my village, my priest concludes that the wrath of God is hanging over the human race ... To see our civil wars, who does not exclaim that the world is turned upside down and that Judgement Day is upon us, without thinking that many worse things have been seen, and that times are good in ten thousand other parts of the world. (1.26)

This remark may be no more than a Christian critique of human presumption for claiming to understand the ways of God. 'Thy judgements are a great deep' (Psalms 36.6, a sentence Montaigne had painted in his study). Alternatively, Montaigne could be denying Providence altogether, along the lines suggested by Lucretius, a Roman poet of the first century BC whose *Nature of the Universe* presents it as a meaningless dance of atoms. We know that Lucretius was one of Montaigne's favourite authors. On the other hand, he may have enjoyed the poem as fiction, without sharing the author's ideas. Once again, Montaigne is opaque. It is easy to see what he is against but difficult to decide what he is for.

Montaigne's defence of witches in one of the best-known of his essays proceeds on similar lines to his discussions of miracles and of Providence. 'The witches of my part of the world are in danger of their life', he wrote, every time anyone takes it into his head to accuse them. Yet, as he drily observed, 'to kill people one needs evidence which is clear and does not admit of doubt' (*A tuer les gens, il faut une clarté lumineuse et nette*) (3.11). This 'luminous' clarity is simply not to be found in the witch-trials, which are full of contradictory evidence. The confessions of the witches are not good enough evidence to condemn them, for, like the accusations, these confessions can sometimes be shown to be inaccurate. Human testimony is to be believed in purely human affairs, but not in cases involving the supernatural. The accused should have been given 'hellebore, not hemlock'. That is, they are sick, not criminals, and in need of a purge to take away the melancholy humour which had made them imagine crimes they had probably not committed. After all, 'It is taking one's conjectures rather seriously to roast someone alive for them' (*c'est mettre ses conjectures à bien haut pris que d'en faire cuire un homme tout vif*) (3.11).

Once again, human presumption is under attack. Montaigne is not necessarily denying the existence of witches, any more than he denies the existence of miracles. What he is calling into doubt is the power of human reason and its 'conjectures' to detect witches. Yet it is hard for the modern reader (at least) not to entertain the idea that witches (and miracles, and even Providence), may not exist at all, and hard not to think that Montaigne, in true Socratic fashion, was not encouraging the reader to do this. Here as elsewhere in the *Essays*, Montaigne gives the impression of wanting readers to draw conclusions which are never explicit in the text. The difficulty for us, four hundred years later, lies in deciding what he expected contemporaries to read between his lines.

The point Montaigne was making openly about witches would have been shocking enough to many people. It was a view close to that of the Italian humanist Andrea Alciati (who had made the crack about hellebore some seventy years earlier), not to mention Montaigne's former colleagues in the parlement of Bordeaux, who had been treating cases of witchcraft as 'false imagination'. However, this view was in complete contradiction to the conventional attitude that witches were a real threat, an attitude expressed by Montaigne's distinguished contemporary Jean Bodin, an almost universal scholar (best known today as a political theorist), in a book published in the same year as the *Essays*, called the *Demonomania*.

Miracles, Providence and witchcraft were not the only religious issues on which Montaigne expressed unconventional opinions. He also compared prayers to spells or charms used for 'magical effects', on the grounds that most people prayed without real devotion; a bold remark at a time when Protestants were criticising the magic of the Catholic Church (1.56). He rehearsed the arguments in favour of suicide, although suicide was forbidden (2.3). He was interested in comparative religion, and pointed out that the ideas of the Flood, the Incarnation and the Virgin Birth are all known outside the Jewish-Christian tradition, together with practices such as the celibacy of the priesthood, fasting and circumcision (2.12).

The last point might seem particularly subversive, but Montaigne turns it to Christian use and explains similarities between Christianity and the religions of the American Indians by supernatural inspiration'. Did he mean what he wrote? What, more generally, was his religious position? We have seen that the *Essays* are both informative and opaque. Montaigne gives us a good deal of information, while making that information difficult to interpret. The problem of interpretation may be posed, for the sake of simplicity, in the form of a dilemma.

The first possibility is that Montaigne was more of a Catholic than a sceptic, a man who entertained all sorts of unorthodox opinions but did not really take them seriously. All he was doing in his book, he claimed more than once, was putting forward his 'fancies' (*fantasies*), in the same way that theses were put forward for disputation in the universities in his day, provisionally, tentatively, 'not to declare the truth but to look for it'. These fancies were, he wrote, 'matters of opinion, not matters of faith: what I think to myself, not what I believe according to God.' They were simply thought-experiments, offered for correction as children offer their exercises', and it was for this reason that he gave them the title, then unusual, of his 'essays' (1.56). Montaigne here seems close to the view of 'double truth' put forward by the sixteenth-century Italian philosopher Pietro Pomponazzi. Pomponazzi argued that there were cases where a given proposition, for example, 'the soul is immortal', is known to be true according to faith but cannot be demonstrated by reason, while its converse is supported by equally strong, or even stronger, rational arguments. Montaigne knew that some of the views he advanced were 'temerarious' (to use the theological term for doctrines which are unorthodox but have not been condemned as heretical), but he declared his willingness to submit to the authority of the Church. When he was in Rome, he did in fact submit the *Essays*, which had just been published, to the papal censor. They were passed with six objections, which cannot have been serious, since Montaigne was told it was up to him whether he corrected them or not, and in fact he did not. The censor found nothing worse than the frequent references to 'fortune' (rather than Providence), the naming of poets who were heretics (like the leading Calvinist Theodore Beza), and the defence of a convert from Christianity, the fourth-century emperor Julian the Apostate. Does the censor's reaction show that we are anachronistic to find Montaigne subversive? It would be a rash historian who claimed to have a sharper nose for heresy than a sixteenth-century papal censor, yet it is difficult not to wonder whether this censor was aware of all the implications of Montaigne's ideas. One reason for his mildness was no doubt the fact that in the 1580s the most serious threat to the Church came from the Protestants. Montaigne was not particularly sympathetic to Protestantism, while scepticism seemed more an ally than an enemy in the fight against heresy. The protestations about mere 'fancies', and the comparison with children's exercises, were no doubt taken quite literally by the censor. But suppose that (like the off-hand remarks about his 'scribblings' elsewhere), they were intended ironically?

The obvious alternative view is that Montaigne was more of a sceptic than a Catholic, and that he never abandoned the principle of suspension of judgement. He once declared that of human opinions on religion (those unsupported by faith), the one with most plausibility (*vraysemblance*) was that which 'recognised God as an incomprehensible power, origin and conserver of all things ... taking in good part the honour and reverence which humans rendered unto him by whatever name and in whatever form' (2.12). Sextus Empiricus recommended the sceptic to follow the customs of his own society, and Montaigne's behaviour is consistent with this advice. When in Rome he did as the pope did. The statements of his submissiveness to ecclesiastical authority can be seen as part of this exterior conformity, practised for purely prudential reasons.

One is reminded of Montaigne's acquaintance the scholar Justus Lipsius, who behaved as a Calvinist when he taught in Leiden, in the Dutch Republic, but as a Catholic when he taught in Louvain, in the Spanish Netherlands. In fact, as we now know, he was a member of a small sect, the Family of Love, which recommended this exterior conformity to all its members. I am not suggesting that Montaigne was a 'Familist' – he may never even have heard of this group – but simply pointing out that there were sixteenth-century Europeans who practised exterior conformity to one form of religion while believing that another was better.

According to this second interpretation of his position, Montaigne was being prudent and insincere when he wrote that it belonged to the Church to tell him what to think, but revealing his true attitude when he declared that 'Society has nothing to do with our thoughts' (*la société publique n'a que faire de nos pensées*), that we all need a 'room at the back of the shop' (*une arrière boutique*), where we can be ourselves, and that 'the wise man ought to retire into himself, and allow himself to judge freely of everything, but outwardly he ought completely to follow the established order' (1.23). Where the 'Catholic' view of Montaigne takes this statement, from the essay 'On custom', as referring to secular matters alone, the 'sceptical' view takes him to be referring to religion as well as politics. This second view seems to make better sense of Montaigne's literary tactics of preferring hints to open statements and of hiding unconventional opinions in essays which appear to be concerned with something quite different. It implies that Montaigne's protestations of frankness were a mask, and that he was one man in public but another in private. The public and the private Montaignes will be discussed in the next two chapters.

5 Montaigne's politics

We have seen that Montaigne's religion is not easy to charac-
terise. His political position does not fit neatly into modern
categories either. Some writers have called him a liberal, others
have reacted against this and labelled him a conservative. Both
terms are anachronistic. The word 'liberal' generally refers to a
package of modern attitudes – approval of democracy, tolera-
tion, the rights of minorities, freedom of speech, and so on –
attitudes which Montaigne did not share. His famous defence of
witches is based not on liberal but on sceptical grounds, on the
fact that the identification of a witch is pure conjecture. He did
not advocate freedom of worship for the French Calvinists of his
day. He opposed the Protestant theory of the Christian's duty to
disobey unjust commands by the ruler: 'It should not be left to
the judgement of the individual to decide where his duty lies. He
must be told what to do' (2.12). Like Socrates and Sextus Empiricus, he advocated outward conformity to the customs of
one's own country.

His support of outward conformity may suggest that Montaigne was a conservative. The difficulty here is that if we want
to use the term in a precise sense, we have to say that a conservative is someone who opposes the liberals. In this sense, no one
was a conservative in the sixteenth century. Right and Left, as
names of specific parties, were born together at the French
Revolution. If we resolve to use the term 'conservative' in a
vaguer sense, we are faced with the opposite problem. In the
weak sense of the word, everyone was a conservative in the
sixteenth century, for everyone, Luther no less than the pope,
defended his views by appealing to tradition.

What we can say is that Montaigne disliked change, whether
or not it was justified by an appeal to the past. He was well aware
that there was much that was wrong with the society in which
he lived. The sale of the office of judge was something which
struck him as particularly absurd (1.23). The 'corruption' or

'sickness' of his age is a recurrent theme in his essays. However, he argued that change was always to be feared. 'In public affairs, there is no course so bad, provided that it is stable and tradition-al, that is not better than change and alteration ... It is easy enough to criticise a political system (*une police*) ... But to establish a better regime in place of the one which has been destroyed, there is the problem' (2.17). His scepticism cut both ways. It condemned revolution no less than repression, and for the same reason. 'It demands a great deal of self-love and presumption, to take one's own opinions so seriously as to dis-rupt the peace in order to establish them, introducing so many inevitable evils, and so terrible a corruption of manners as civil wars and political revolutions (*mutations d'estat*) bring with them' (1.23).

There we have it. Montaigne was not simply drawing the consequences of scepticism, but thinking about the civil wars, which were at the centre of his reflections on politics, as they had to be for a Frenchman of his generation. Historians often distin-guish four civil wars in France in the second half of the sixteenth century, but in practice the whole period from 1562 (the date of the massacre of Vassy and the battle of Dreux), to 1595 (when the pope absolved Henri IV), was one of continual war. 'Religious' wars they are called, with Catholics on one side and Calvinists, known as 'Huguenots', on the other. The Huguenots, who included noblemen (and noblewomen), lawyers, merchants and craftsmen, were particularly strong in the towns of the south, including Bordeaux. The government, or more precisely the regent, Catherine de'Medici, and the chancellor, Michel de l'Hôpital, began by making concessions to the Huguenots who were given freedom of worship in 1562. As the Huguenots grew stronger, the government's attitude changed. The notorious Massacre of St Bartholomew of 1572 began as an attempt by Catherine de'Medici to have the Huguenot leader, Admiral Coligny, assassinated, but it quickly developed into a massacre of the Protestants in Paris, an example soon imitated at Lyons, Toulouse, Bordeaux and elsewhere. When Catherine returned to a policy of concessions to the Huguenots, she provoked a Catholic reaction. It was at local, popular level that intolerance could be found. The formation of a 'Catholic League' on a nation-wide scale, in 1576, to defend the interests of the Catholics, who felt themselves betrayed by the government, followed the establishment of local leagues of the same kind.

Why did the Catholic majority hate the Protestant minority with such violence? People were not yet used to religious diversity in this period, and they felt threatened by it. Most French Catholics (though not Montaigne) hated and feared Huguenots as they hated and feared Jews, Turks and witches (and as English Protestants hated and feared 'Papists'). The Massacre of St Bartholomew was an attempt to appease God and purify the community by destroying nonconformists. Such attitudes were not universal – Montaigne was on good terms with the Protestant gentry of his neighbourhood – but they were common, and this was one of the main reasons for the civil wars.

These wars also had a political dimension. The great nobles, like the Guises and the Bourbons, did not create the situation, but they did exploit it, in their natural conflict of interest with a monarchy which had recently been pursuing policies of centralisation at their expense. The Guises put themselves at the head of the Catholic League, while the Bourbons supported the Huguenots, who created a federal state of their own, in the Swiss style, in Languedoc. These great nobles made religion a 'cloak' to cover their ambition, according to the *politiques*, a third force which emerged in the course of the civil wars and tried to put an end to them. Jean Bodin was one member of this group; Montaigne was another. He once remarked that both Henri Duke of Guise and the Bourbon Henri of Navarre (later Henri IV), advocated in public, for political reasons, the exact opposite of their true religious beliefs: 'For Navarre, if he did not fear to be deserted by his followers, would be ready to return of his own accord to the religion of his forefathers; and Guise, if there were no danger, would not be averse to the Augsburg Confession'. He doubted whether all those who fought for nothing but religious or patriotic motives would together make 'a complete company of armed men', let alone an army. High motives concealed low ones. 'Our zeal works wonders, whenever it supports our inclination toward hatred, cruelty, ambition' (2.12). He thought the better party 'that which maintains the ancient religion and constitution of the country' (*la religion et la police ancienne du pays*) (2.19), but he tried to pursue a middle course in the wars, with all the 'inconveniences', as he put it, 'that moderation brings in such illnesses'. With a wry reference to the faction-fighting of medieval Italy he added 'To the Ghibellines I was a Guelph, to the Guelphs a Ghibelline' (3.12).

The French civil wars encouraged men to rethink their polit-ical theory, as civil wars often do. It concentrates the mind wonderfully on the question where power lies (or ought to lie), when that power is being used to destroy something that one values. From the point of view of the political theorist, the wars were a conflict between two views of kingship. The first was the view that the power of the king comes from the people, that this power is limited, and that in certain circumstances rebellion against the 'tyrant' is justified. This was the view of the Huguenots after the Massacre of St Bartholomew, as expressed, for example, in the pseudonymous *Defence of Liberty against Tyrants* (1579). A similar position was taken up in *The Law of the Kingdom in Scotland*, a treatise by Montaigne's old teacher George Buchanan, written about the year 1570 to justify the deposition of Mary Queen of Scots (1568), but published in 1579 because of its relevance to the situation in France. In the 1580s, a similar view of the right of resistance to tyrants was put forward by supporters of the Catholic League. Extremes met.

The alternative was the theory that the power of the king comes from God, not from the people; that this power is not shared or limited but 'absolute' (*puissance absolue*); and consequently that rebellion is never justified. This was the view of Adam Blackwood, a Scot living in France who answered his compatriot Buchanan with an *Apologia for Kings* (1581). The idea that sovereignty is indivisible received powerful support from Jean Bodin.

Montaigne never put forward anything as systematic as a political theory. Despite the description of the essays by their first English translator, Florio (following the Italian version), as 'Moralle, Politike and Millitarie Discourses', few of them deal directly with political questions. All the same, Montaigne was well aware of contemporary controversies over the nature and limits of monarchy. The latest books were clearly reaching him in his tower. He commented with amused detachment on Buchanan and Blackwood: 'Less than a month ago, I was leafing through two Scottish books which took up opposite positions on this subject. The democrat (*le populaire*) puts the king lower than a carter; the monarchist places him well above God in power and sovereignty' (3.7).

Montaigne found the two Scotsmen amusing because he thought disputes about the best form of government or society to be of no practical value, conjectures 'fit for nothing but the exercise of our wit' (3.9). He was no utopian. In politics as in religion he had an acute sense of the limits of human reason. Like Machiavelli, he was well aware of the importance of the incalculable in human affairs, a force they both described as 'Fortune'. Like Machiavelli, he thought it necessary, on occasion, for princes 'to use bad means to a good end'. However, he had his reservations about Machiavelli. The *Discourses* he described as 'very solid', so far as the subject allowed; 'but it has been extremely easy to criticise them, and those who have done so have been equally open to criticism.' Machiavelli's belief in general rules 'which rarely or never fail' did not appeal to Montaigne, who considered political forecasts to be about as unreliable as weather forecasts – he was thinking of the almanacs and prognostications of his day; to do the exact opposite of what they recommend, he declared, is no more imprudent than to trust them (2.17). By different means one may arrive at the same result, and by the same means, at different results. The Emperor Julian the Apostate used 'the same recipe of liberty of conscience, to kindle civil war, which our kings have just employed to extinguish it' (2.19). That particular remark may be a covert critique of the rulers of his day, but Montaigne's acute awareness of diversity always made him extremely sceptical of generalisations.

In principle, therefore, Montaigne was no supporter of monarchy, aristocracy or democracy. His views were pragmatic and relativist. Unlike many of his contemporaries he did not believe in an eternal immutable 'law of nature' underlying actual law; the diversity of human customs was too great for that. He thought that monarchy was best for France, but that different political regimes were appropriate to different societies, precisely because of the power of custom. 'Peoples who are brought up in liberty and self-government regard all other regimes as monstrous and unnatural. Those who are accustomed to monarchy do the same' (1.23). This is a view not far from that of Machiavelli, who recognised the difficulty for a prince to become master of a city which had been accustomed to freedom, but Montaigne's conclusions about human diversity are taken much further than Machiavelli wanted to take them.

The most excellent and best regime for any nation is that under which it has maintained itself. Its essential form and utility depends on usage. We are easily displeased with the system we have, but all the same I hold that it is wicked and stupid to wish for the rule of the few in a democracy, or in a monarchy, another kind of regime. (3.9)

Or again, with the simplicity and immediacy of a proverb, 'Let every foot have its own shoe' (3.13).

In short, Montaigne wanted to maintain the traditional political order, but for untraditional reasons, reasons which he expresses on occasion with an unusual and brutal (not to say cynical) frankness, which may remind the modern reader of Hobbes. 'The laws are maintained in credit, not because they are just, but because they are laws. That is the mystical foundation of their authority; they have no other' (3.13). For Montaigne, the study of other cultures and the 'legitimation crisis', the conflict over authority through which France was passing during the civil wars (and through which England would pass in Hobbes's day), demystified the law. It was clear to Montaigne both that specific laws were arbitrary, not natural, and that these laws must not be questioned, but obeyed.

The civil wars also demystified the monarchy. Many Frenchmen of the day believed in their king's power to work miracles, more particularly to cure sufferers from scrofula by the virtue of the royal touch. Even members of the *politique* group, like the lawyer Etienne Pasquier, argued that it was necessary to regard

the monarch as 'sacrosanct, inviolable and holy'. Like his friend
La Boétie, Montaigne seems to have thought otherwise. La
Boétie wrote a treatise which was critical of monarchy in general
and the 'miracles' of the French kings in particular. He
described public rituals as 'drugs' to make the people sub-
missive (an idea which is not far removed from Marx's description of religion as the opium of the people). Unlike La Boétie,
Montaigne was, as we have seen, no enemy of the institution of
monarchy, but like him he seems to have felt the need to strip
away illusions from it, to show that the emperor has no clothes,
or rather, that it is only his clothes which make him different
from the rest of us. 'Why do people respect the package rather
than the man?' (*Pourquoy, estimant un homme, l'estimez vous tout
enveloppé et empaqueté?*) 'the Emperor, whose pomp dazzles you
in public . . . look at him behind the curtain, and you see nothing
but an ordinary man' (1.42). Elsewhere he points out that 'the
souls of emperors and cobblers are all cast in the same mould'
(2.12), and that 'even if we sit on the highest throne in the world,
we are still sitting on our own bottom' (*au plus eslevé throne du
monde, si ne sommes assis que sus nostre cul* : 3.13). Montaigne was
of course well aware that kings are not the only people to play
social roles. Clothes, custom and ceremony support not only the
monarchy but the whole social hierarchy. It is much easier for
us to imagine a craftsman 'upon his close stool or upon his wife'
than a president of a parlement in the same position, because he
appears in public dressed in splendid robes (3.2). Unlike some
of his contemporaries, Montaigne did not want to overturn the
social and political order. However, he did not want people to
have illusions about it either.

In his wish to strip public life bare of pretence, Montaigne
was, like La Boétie, a moralist in the stoic tradition. Marcus
Aurelius (AD 121–80), although an emperor himself, had a view
of the profession which was not far from Montaigne's. In his
Meditations, he wrote that 'where there are things which appear
most worthy of our approbation, we ought to lay them bare and
look at their worthlessness and strip them of all the words with
which they are exalted. For outward show is a wonderful

perverter of the reason.' The unmasking of public life is the reverse of Montaigne's praise of private life, to which we must now turn.

6 Montaigne as psychologist

Montaigne retired to his tower because he was tired of public office and public life. He wanted solitude and tranquillity of mind. Marcus Aurelius had written that there was no need for seekers of tranquillity to retreat to a house in the country, 'for it is in your power to retire into yourself whenever you choose.' Montaigne, who was aware of this objection, admitted that 'true solitude' was a state of mind, and that it might be enjoyed 'even in the midst of towns or courts', but, he added, 'it may be enjoyed more conveniently away from them.' The important thing was not to give oneself up completely to public affairs (or, indeed, to domestic affairs), but to have a back room for ourselves alone (*une arrière boutique toute nostre*); 'wholly ours, and wholly free, for the sake of our true liberty, as if we lacked wife, children, goods, followers and servants' (1.39).

Montaigne's taste for privacy is not difficult to appreciate today. For a sixteenth-century French gentleman, however, it was unusual in its intensity. Admitting, at least on occasion, that the most honourable occupation is 'to serve the commonwealth, and be profitable to many', he declared his own intention to live a life which was simply 'pardonable', 'burdensome neither to myself nor to anyone else'. After all, he had no head for business, and in any case, he was old (3.9). After living for others it was time to live 'these remains of life' for himself (1.39). So far Montaigne was expressing a relatively conventional rejection of *negotium* for *otium*, but he went further. On two occasions in the essays, he makes clear his distaste for the public death-bed scene which was conventional at the time, complete with 'the wailing of mothers, wives and children . . . a dark room; tapers burning; our bed beset by physicians and preachers' (1.20). ' I have seen a number of dying men, most pitiably beset by all this throng; it stifles them . . . I am content with a death . . . quiet and solitary, wholly mine, appropriate to my retiring and private life . . . there is no role for society in this scene; it is an act for one character alone' (3.9). For many of his contemporaries, on the contrary, what was pitiable was to die alone. Here as elsewhere in his essays, Montaigne shows his preoccupation with death and how to meet it. Preoccupation, not obsession; a concern with the 'art of dying well' was no personal peculiarity but a characteristic of his age. Death was not yet taboo.

Montaigne's preference for solitude was more personal. Yet it was not a preference of the same order as his taste for fish, which he tells us was his favourite food. Montaigne believed in private life while he did not believe in public life, at least not in his own troubled times. He was no civic humanist. Quoting the saying that 'we are not born for our private good, but for the public', he went on to suggest that this sentiment was no more than a cover for 'ambition and avarice', and that men really sought public office for private profit (1.39). The more fools they, for 'Of all the follies of the world, the most widely accepted and most universal is the care for reputation and glory' (1.41). There can be no doubt what Montaigne would have thought of Louis XIV or Napoleon. It is true that he did admire Alexander the Great, but not in an unqualified way. He thought Socrates the greater man.

> I can easily imagine Socrates in Alexander's place, but not Alexander in that of Socrates. If anyone asks Alexander what he can do, he will reply, 'Conquer the world'. Socrates will answer the same question, 'Lead my life in a manner befitting its natural condition'; a form of knowledge more general, more important, and more legitimate. (3.2)

It seems, then, that Montaigne was being ironic when he made his excuses for retiring to his ivory tower. He did not really see withdrawal from public life as escapism. On the contrary, he thought private life more challenging. He equated the private realm with the natural, and the public realm with the artificial, as his recurrent use of imagery from the theatre reveals.

> Anyone may ... represent an honourable man upon the stage; but to follow a rule within oneself, where everything is possible, and every-thing hidden, that's the real problem ... we who live a private life not exposed to any gaze but our own need to have a touch-stone in our hearts to determine the quality of our actions ... I have my own laws and my own court to judge myself. (3.2)

Like Socrates, whose famous 'demon' was a kind of interior oracle, Montaigne was advocating what an American sociologist has called 'inner-direction', as opposed to the uncritical acceptance of traditional norms of behaviour or the standards of one's peers. He was undermining the dominant noble ethic of the time, the ethic of honour, based on 'the approbation of others . . . a much too uncertain and unstable foundation' (3.2). To follow the 'inner light' in this way was not an odd claim to make in sixteenth-century Europe (not in Protestant circles, at least), but it was unusual to make this claim in secular terms and in a secular context, as Montaigne was doing here.

If the true man is the man off-stage, behind the curtain, it follows that we need to study the private life of the heroes of antiquity. Unfortunately, classical and Renaissance notions of the 'dignity of history' excluded intimate details from the record. Montaigne has some sharp and penetrating criticisms of historians, ancient and modern, who all too often 'select the matters which they consider most worthy to be known and conceal a word or a private action which would reveal much more'. Montaigne would rather have known what Brutus talked about 'in his tent with some of his close friends, the night before a battle, than the speech he made to his army the next day; and what he did in his chamber, or closet, than in the Forum or the Senate' (2.10).

For this reason Montaigne preferred biography to history. As the French bishop Amyot put it in the preface to his translation of Plutarch's *Lives*, one of Montaigne's favourite books, 'the one [history] is more concerned with things, the other [biography] with persons; the one is more public, the other more private; the one more concerned with what is outside, the other with what comes from within; the one with events, the other with the reasons for actions.' Montaigne does not seem to have known the *Lives of Illustrious Men* by the sixteenth-century humanist bishop Paolo Giovio, or Vasari's lives of Italian artists, published in 1550. However, he did know his Plutarch, he did read the *Lives of the Caesars* by Suetonius (*c.* 69–*c.* 140 AD), and he did appreciate the *Lives of the Philosophers* by the third-century Greek writer Diogenes Laertius, who tells us, for example, not only that Zeno was the founder of the Stoics, but also that he came from Cyprus and was fond of fresh figs.

Trivia? Not for Montaigne, who believed that a man's character was expressed in such apparently unimportant details, just as it was made manifest, to those who had eyes to see, by the habitual and unconscious movements of the body. 'Every movement reveals us (*tout mouvement nous descouvre*). The very same mind of Caesar, which we see in the order and direction of the battle of Pharsalia, is also visible in the planning of his leisure and his love affairs' (1.50). And again: 'Our body easily retains some impression of our natural inclinations, involuntarily and unconsciously (*sans nostre sceu et consentement*) . . . Julius Caesar used to scratch his head with his finger, which is the gesture of a man oppressed by painful thoughts; and Cicero, as I recall, had a tic of wrinkling his nose, which is the sign of a scoffing nature' (2.17). Their body language spoke volumes. Montaigne also believed that dreams revealed the dreamer's wishes. In his essay 'on the force of the imagination', he also discussed the possibility of a psychological explanation for the stigmata of St Francis and for the cures effected by the royal touch (1.21). He rejected the claims of the diviners, but he did not reject the possibility of reading signs. What he did was to interpret these signs in a naturalistic manner.

It is not difficult to see why Sigmund Freud should have read Montaigne with attention. They agreed about dreams and about the importance of the earliest years, when habits are formed: 'our greatest vices take root in our most tender infancy and the most important part of our education is in the hands of nurses' (1.23). Like Freud, Montaigne saw himself as a lone explorer of the self, a pioneer in the 'thorny enterprise (more difficult than it looks), of following a path as wandering as that of the mind and of penetrating the dark depths of its inner folds' (2.6).

However, we should not take the self-image of the lone explorer too seriously in either case. Original as they both were, neither man really cut himself loose from the traditions of his culture. What Montaigne did was to create a personal synthesis from the insights expressed in medical, philosophical, rhetorical and theological traditions which went back to the ancient

Greeks. Hippocrates (*c.* 460–380 BC) formulated rules for diag-
nosing illness from symptoms. Aristotle's *Rhetoric* discusses the
symptoms of emotion. To diagnose personality from symptoms
was the next step, taken, at the latest, by Theophrastus (*c.* 372–
c. 288 BC), a pupil of Aristotle's and the author of the *Characters*,
a set of vivid vignettes of 'the boor', 'the superstitious man', and
so on. These ideas were part of the cultural context of the
biographies by Plutarch and Diogenes Laertius, on whom Montaigne drew so freely. In his own day, artists, playwrights and
actors were all well aware of the symptoms of emotion and
character, and some physicians, notably in their studies of
melancholy, were formulating the laws of what we call 'psychology'. The term 'psychology' was in fact coined in the sixteenth
century, but had no success till the eighteenth. In his discussion
of the outward signs of personality, as in other parts of his
essays, Montaigne was not making a suggestion which was completely unthinkable by his contemporaries, but rather picking
up an idea which, though current, ran counter to the conventional belief in the dignity of history, taking it more seriously,
exploring its implications more thoroughly and developing it
further than anyone else.

A similar point might be made about Montaigne's analysis of
what Freud called 'rationalisation', our propensity to credit ourselves with better motives than true self-knowledge would
allow. *Piperie*, 'cheating', is his favourite word for it. Where
Calvin, for example, had discussed self-deception in religious
terms, Montaigne's analysis is essentially secular. We have seen
that the *politiques* argued that religion was a rationalisation, or
in their more vivid phrase, a 'cloak' for many selfish designs.
Montaigne, however, went much further in his analysis of
piperie, and his essays have a place between the *Confessions* of St
Augustine (a book he seems not to have known), and the *Maxims*
of La Rochefoucauld (who knew the *Essays* well), as a classic
exposure of the workings of self-love and hypocrisy. He was well
aware that zeal for the public good may conceal ambition (1.39);
that a man may be humble out of pride (2.17); that the public
profession of virtue may mask a vicious private life (3.5), and,
more generally, that there is often a gap between a man's in-

dividual weaknesses and his public 'role' (*role* is a term which occurs several times in the *Essays* in this sense). It is scarcely surprising that no man is a hero to his valet, or more exactly, in Montaigne's version of the epigram, that *peu d'hommes ont esté admirez par leurs domestiques* (3.2).

Given his desire for total honesty and his awareness of the masks which others wear, Montaigne could deal with some of his central themes only by discussing himself. 'Other people do not see you at all, but guess at you by uncertain conjectures' (3.2). The apparent digressions into the details of his private life, his health, his colic, his idiosyncrasies in food and clothes, digressions which irritated contemporary readers, are there for epistemological reasons, on the grounds that 'every man embodies the whole pattern of the human condition' (*chaque homme porte la forme entiere de l'humaine condition*) (3.2). *Forme* seems to be used in this passage in the Aristotelian sense of the design embedded in matter. Montaigne in his tower has something important in common with Descartes in his stove, or with Proust observing himself on his death-bed. His detailed description of his sensations after falling from his horse reads like the account of an experiment designed to discover what it feels like to die (2.6). This crucial epistemological point is partly disguised by Montaigne's characteristic presentation of the autobiographical passages as nothing but harmless self-indulgence. He noted that King René of Anjou had painted a self-portrait: 'Why is it not as legitimate' (he added), 'for every man to portray himself with his pen, as it was for him to do it with a crayon?' (2.17).

Montaigne knew that autobiography had been tried before, though, curiously enough, he cannot have been aware of its development in Renaissance Italy. The autobiographies of Pope Pius II (writing in the 1460s), Benvenuto Cellini (writing in the 1560s), and the Milanese physician Girolamo Cardano (writing in 1575), ran parallel to the rise of the self-portrait in the same region and the same period (Pinturicchio, Vasari and Titian, for example). The affinities between Cardano's presentation of himself and Montaigne's are particularly striking. Cardano's book includes chapters on his health, his appearance ('a rather too shrill voice ... a fixed gaze, as if in meditation'), and 'those things in which I take pleasure', including fishing, solitude and reading history. However, none of the three Italian autobiographies was in print at the time that Montaigne was writing. The coincidence in time between Cellini, Cardano and Montaigne suggests that awareness of individuality is a social phenomenon.

Of a piece with his frankness in other respects was Montaigne's attitude to sex, *l'action genitale* as he called it. One of his essays, 'On the force of the imagination', is essentially concerned with impotence, which he interpreted in psychological terms and not, like so many of his contemporaries, as the result of sorcery. Montaigne explained impotence by anxiety and consequent self-consciousness which inhibits action, noting, here as in his discussion of nervous tics, the independence of our bodies from our will (1.21).

His most extended discussion of sexuality occurs in the essay 'On some verses of Virgil' (highly explicit verses from the eighth book of the *Aeneid*, describing Venus and Vulcan making love). The essay raised the problem of the sex taboo in Montaigne's own culture, a taboo which he found extremely odd:

Why was the act of generation made so natural, so necessary and so right, if we dare not speak of it without embarrassment, and exclude it from serious conversation? We are bold enough to pronounce words like kill, rob, betray; but this word we only speak under our breath . . . Are we not brutes to call 'brutish' the act which engenders us? (3.5)

How recent the taboo was in Montaigne's day is difficult to say. There are some grounds for suggesting that it was growing stronger in the later sixteenth century than it had been in the age of Rabelais. In Montaigne's day, as he pointed out in this essay, a pope could be shocked by the nudity of Rome's population of classical statues.

What is striking about this particular essay is, first, Montaigne's determination to discuss, coolly and publicly, what had become the most private of subjects (many of his contemporaries broke the taboo, but no one else, to my knowledge, discussed it), and second, his comparative approach. He discusses attitudes to sexuality in different cultures; parts of the world where nudity is the norm, where there is a cult of the phallus, or where eating is an activity with the same associations of shame and privacy that sex has for us. Montaigne views this panorama of human diversity with a serene and ironic curiosity. His general attitude to other cultures is the subject of the next chapter.

One of the most striking characteristics of Montaigne – for us late-twentieth-century readers at least – is the breadth and depth of his interest in other cultures, his freedom from ethnocentrism combined with an acute awareness of the ethnocentrism of others. His essay on custom lists society after society where what Europeans would consider odd, funny, or shocking is treated as normal: 'where virgins show their private parts openly ... where there are male prostitutes ... where women go to war ... where women piss standing up, and men squat', and he concludes that 'The laws of conscience, which we say derive from nature, derive from custom ... whatever is beyond the compass of custom is thought to be beyond the compass of reason' (1.23).

Still more famous is his essay on cannibals, which gives a detailed description of some of the newly-discovered Indians of Brazil; their food, their long-houses, their songs and dances. Montaigne notes that these Brazilians had 'no trade, no knowledge of writing, no arithmetic, no magistrate, no political subordination ... no riches or poverty, no contracts, no inheritance ... no clothes, no agriculture, no metal.' However, he refuses to call them barbarians or savages. They are 'wild' (*sauvages*) only in the sense that we call certain fruits 'wild' – because they are natural, not domesticated (1.31).

After reading passages like these, one is tempted to describe Montaigne as an anthropologist, or at least as a 'precursor' of modern social anthropology. The danger in doing this is that of failing to discriminate between the cultural context in which the discipline of social anthropology was founded, at the end of the nineteenth century, and that of Montaigne's day. He was writing as a moralist; modern anthropologists, generally speaking, do not. For this reason the word 'anthropologist' will be replaced, throughout this chapter, by the vaguer term 'ethnographer'.

Ethnography, in the sense of curiosity about exotic customs, was certainly flourishing in Montaigne's day. Such curiosity had not been unusual in the later Middle Ages, as Marco Polo's account of China will remind us, or the travels of 'Mandeville', which were fictional but taken as factual and were apparently widely read. In the sixteenth century, the interest in the exotic seems to have become still stronger, witness the popularity of the *Customs of Different Nations* (1520), compiled by Johann Boehm, canon of Ulm.

There are two obvious reasons for the trend. The first is the revival of classical antiquity. The ancient Greeks had shown great interest in other cultures. Socrates, as Montaigne reminds us, treated the whole world as his native city, and the stoics had similar cosmopolitan ideals. Herodotus, who was much studied in the sixteenth century, had a keen eye for ethnographic detail; it was he who recorded the fact that in Egypt, unlike Greece, it was the women who carried loads on their heads and passed water standing up. Besides details of exotic customs, the classics offered conceptual schemata for interpreting them. Sixteenth-century writers who discussed whether the American Indians were 'slaves by nature', or whether they were still living in the golden age, before the introduction of private property, were looking at the Indians through classical eyes.

The interest in alien customs was also encouraged, naturally enough, by the discovery of America. Books about the discovery often devote chapters to the way of life of the Indians, whether the attitude of the author is sympathetic, hostile, or neutral. A well-known example is the *General History of the Indies* (1552), by the Spanish cleric Francisco López de Gómara. The dedication of the history to the emperor Charles V sums up Gómara's attitude. Before the Spaniards arrived, he declares, the Indians were idolaters, cannibals and sodomites. He interprets the conquest of the New World and the conversion of its inhabitants to Christianity and the Spanish way of life as the work of God. It should be added that the author was in the service of Hernán Cortés, the conqueror of Mexico.

Gómara was an apologist for Spanish conquest in general and that of Cortés in particular. A very different account of Indian customs emerges from the *History of the New World* (1565) by Girolamo Benzoni. A Milanese, hence himself subject to Spanish rule, Benzoni, who had spent fourteen years in the New World, condemns the cruelty of the Spaniards and gives a detailed and sympathetic description of the Indian way of life.

Montaigne's Brazilians had been studied in particular detail in the twenty years or so before he wrote. A German, Hans Staden, had been captured by the Tupinamba and learned their language while waiting to be eaten, but escaped to publish a curiously detached account of their customs in 1557. Montaigne does not seem to have known about Staden's book, but he did know accounts of Brazil by two French visitors, André Thevet and Jean de Léry. Thevet was a Franciscan. His *Singularities of Antarctic France* (1558) showed considerable interest in the 'way of life' (*manière de vivre*) of the inhabitants of Brazil. He thought that they lived 'like beasts' (*brutalement*). All the same, the comparison between Brazil and 'our Europe', as Thevet calls it, is not altogether to our advantage. Idolatrous as they are, the Brazilians are better than the 'damnable atheists of our time'. A similar point was made by the French Protestant Jean de Léry in his *Story of a Voyage to Brazil* (1578). Léry thought the Brazilians barbarians who illustrated the corruption of human nature after the Fall. At the same time, he emphasised what he called their 'humanity', and declared that their peace, harmony and charity put Christians to shame at a time when innocent people were being massacred in France.

In his *Germania*, the great Roman historian Tacitus (first century AD) had described the courage and the simple manly life of the German barbarians as a reproach to his effeminate contemporaries. In a similar way, Léry used the Brazilians to condemn the St Bartholomew's Day massacre and other atrocities of the French religious wars. We might call this technique the 'Germania syndrome'. It can also be found in Ronsard, who declared his wish to leave France and its troubles for the Antarctic, 'where savages live and happily follow the law of nature', and in La Boétie, who wrote a Latin poem lamenting the civil wars and expressing a desire to start life afresh in the New World.

At this point we may return to Montaigne, to whom La Boétie's poem was addressed, and ask how he differed from these contemporaries. Montaigne read Gómara, Benzoni, Thevet and Léry. What he took from Gómara was information, not ideas. Where Gómara had celebrated the Spanish conquest of America, Montaigne, in his essay on coaches, denounced it: 'So many cities razed to the ground; so many nations exterminated; so many millions of people put to the sword; and the richest and fairest part of the world turned upside down for the sake of the trade in pearls and pepper: Base victories.' (3.6). The Spaniards had sometimes pointed to the Indians' cannibalism as a justification for enslaving them. Montaigne's apologia for the cannibals is in part a critique of Spanish policy. He is closer to his compatriots Thevet and Léry than he is to Gómara. Like Léry, he exemplifies the 'Germania syndrome' and uses the Brazilians as a stick to beat his own society as well as to beat Spain. He treats cannibalism on the level of the mote in the neighbour's eye. 'I am not sorry that we note the horrid barbarity of such an action, but I am sorry that, judging their faults correctly, we should be so blind to our own. I think that there is more barbarity in eating a man alive, than in eating him when he is dead.' Like Léry, Montaigne goes on to comment on the cruelty of the French wars of religion (1.31).

Montaigne wrote as a moralist, not a social scientist. He wanted to influence his readers behaviour and he used nations as his *exempla*. He recommended travel as one of the best methods of education – moral education. ' So many humours, sects, judgements, opinions, laws and customs teach us to judge sensibly of our own', to see beyond the end of our noses and recognise the limitations of our reason (1.26).

Shortly after the publication of books one and two of the *Essays*, in 1580, Montaigne went travelling himself, in Germany, Switzerland and Italy. It is interesting to see him practising what he preached. His journal shows the trouble he took to enquire, everywhere he went, into the local customs and beliefs. In Germany, he questioned the Lutherans about their theology; in Switzerland, the Zwinglians and the Calvinists. In Verona, he visited a synagogue and asked the Jews about their rituals. He also went to High Mass in the cathedral there and noted – for once with surprise – how the Italian men stood talking with their backs to the altar and their hats on their heads during the service. In Tuscany, he questioned a peasant woman who had a reputation as a poet, and asked her to compose verses for him. In Rome, he went to a circumcision, an exorcism and a procession of flagellants, noting – from the condition of their footwear – that the flagellants were poor people who probably whipped themselves for money. His ethnographical eye also observed the crowds. 'Walking in the streets', he commented, 'is one of the most common activities of the Romans.' In France he had once interviewed a Brazilian (through an interpreter), and, on another occasion, a dozen witches; but it was Italy which gave Montaigne his best opportunities for fieldwork. In these enquiries we see the practical sceptic, who wants to investigate everything for himself, rather than the metaphysical sceptic, who doubts the evidence of his own senses.

Montaigne did not simply observe, he participated, eating in the local style wherever he went, ' to experience to the full the diversity of manners and customs' (*pour essayer tout à faict la diversité des moeurs et façons*). He uses the word *essayer* in the same sense as his *Essays*. Other travellers of the period paid attention to the local customs, thanks to the growing interest in the exotic. What was distinctive about Montaigne was that his ethnography was reflexive. He made fun of the parochialism of people who took laws to be universal which were no more than 'municipal' (2.12). He approached all customs in the same way, whether they were Brazilian, Roman or Gascon. 'Everyone calls barbarous whatever is not customary with him' (*Chacun appelle barbarie ce qui n'est pas de son usage*) (1.31). Yet 'every custom has its function' (*chaque usage a sa raison*) (3.9). Here Montaigne sounds not unlike a modern functionalist sociologist or anthropologist. This is not really surprising, since, consciously or unconsciously, both he and they draw on an Aristotelian tradition. Everything, according to Aristotle, seeks its own conservation, and everything has a function or 'final cause'. This belief of Montaigne's underlies his opposition to change in the law. He thought it better to trust custom than fallible human reason.

It is in this sense that Montaigne was a relativist. He explored relativism most fully in his 'Apologia for Raymond Sebond'. There he pointed out that there are no universal standards of human beauty. 'The Indians think of it as black, with thick lips and a flat nose ... In Peru, the biggest ears are the most beautiful, and they stretch them as far as they can.' He made a similar point about religion: ' we are Christians by the same title that we are either Perigordins or Germans', though we cheerfully assume that the views we hold as a result of this accident must be the right ones (2.12). Elsewhere in his essays, Montaigne made a similar point about the position of women. As we have seen, he was aware that societies existed where men were prostitutes and women went to war. He concluded that 'Males and females are cast in the same mould: there is little difference between them except by education and custom.' The authority of men over women derived not from nature but from 'usurpation' (3.5).

Almost equally bold were his scattered remarks about ordinary people. He had, for a French noble of his day, an unusual capacity for admiring ordinary people, as well as for sympathising with their sufferings in that age of witch-trials and civil wars. Ordinary people (*le vulgaire*) were, he thought, ignorant and easily misled by appearances, but also spontaneous, close to nature, and so, on occasion, fine examples of patience, constancy and wisdom, without benefit of Aristotle or Cicero. 'I have seen in my time a hundred craftsmen, a hundred peasants who were wiser and happier than rectors of the university, and whom I would rather have resembled' (2.12). They had, by instinct, the right attitude to death. 'I have never seen one of my peasant neighbours worrying about how he would pass his last hour. Nature teaches him not to think about death until he dies' (3.12). Montaigne's ethnography began at home.

Montaigne went further still and criticised ethnocentrism at the level of the whole human race. 'Man creates his image of divinity according to its relation to himself (*selon la relation à soy*) ... man can only imagine according to his capacity.' He questioned the smug assumption of human superiority to animals. 'When I play with my cat, who knows whether she is amusing herself with me, rather than I with her?' (2.12). Of

course this remark has to be taken in context. As we have seen
(p.12 above), Montaigne was using Plutarch's stories about the
wisdom of animals as a way of attacking complacent assumptions about the dignity and rationality of man. However, this
view of animals as a group with as much right to judge us as
we have to judge them follows from his general relativist views.
One might say that he regarded animals as another culture, if
his admiration for them were not part of his admiration for
nature.

It has already been pointed out that Montaigne was not the
first person to be aware of the variety of human customs, beliefs
and norms. Nor was he the first to draw relativist conclusions
from this observation. The presocratic philosopher Xeno-
phanes, who flourished *c.* 530 BC, noted that 'Ethiopians have
gods with snub noses and black hair, Thracians have gods with
grey eyes and red hair', and he concluded (in a passage quoted
by Montaigne), that 'if oxen and horses could draw ... horses
would draw pictures of gods like horses, and oxen of gods like
oxen.' Sextus Empiricus opposed custom to custom as he opposed statement to statement, and suspended judgement. Boc-
caccio told the story of the three rings, symbolising the three
laws given by God to the Jews, the Christians and the Muslims,
each people thinking it had the true one, 'but the question
remains, which of them is right' (*Decameron*, 1.3). In late-
sixteenth-century France, the ideological wars encouraged
relativism, as they encouraged admiration for other, happier
cultures.

Montaigne reacted in both ways on different occasions, for he
was not a thoroughgoing relativist. Sometimes he wrote from
the point of view of his own culture, declaring, for example, that
'the most useful and honourable skill and occupation for a
woman is that of household management', as if unaware of dif-
ferences in the sexual division of labour (3.9). At times he tried
to arbitrate between cultures, as in his suggestion that the
Italians gave women too little freedom but the French too much
(3.5). At other times he treated different cultures as equally
good. On other occasions he criticised culture itself from the
standpoint of nature, arguing that the Indians were better than

the Europeans because 'we have abandoned nature' while they lived close to her (3.12).

Such inconsistencies would be worrying if Montaigne claimed to be a systematic philosopher. He did not. Like his admired Socrates, his function was to be a gadfly, and to sow doubt where there had been complacency. We may say that he was less tightly laced into his own culture than most of his contemporaries – and most of us – and drew more far-reaching consequences than most from his reflections on human variety. With his remarkable gift for seeing the other's point of view – even the cat's – he took pains to record the impression made by French culture on three Brazilians; their surprise that armed men 'would submit to obeying a child' (Charles IX), and also that the poor begged at the gates of the rich 'and did not take the others by the throat, or set fire to their houses' (1.31). Montaigne drew the subversive consequences of the insight that the Brazilians found the French at least as odd as the French found them. In a period when many artists believed in an ideal beauty which could be calculated mathematically, he observed that this ideal was a purely local one, and he was prepared to make a similar point about Christianity. At a time when Europeans were congratulating themselves on their discovery of printing and gunpowder, he reminded them that 'other men, at the other end of the world, in China, had enjoyed them a thousand years earlier' (3.6). Lacking the customary ethnocentrism, Montaigne's attitude to history could scarcely be conventional either.

8 Montaigne as historian

Montaigne's awareness of human diversity extended over time as well as over space. Among his favourite books were the histories of Herodotus, Livy and Tacitus, Caesar's *Commentaries* (in other words, his memoirs), and Plutarch's *Lives*. He also appreciated Froissart's chronicle of the Hundred Years' War, and that of Commynes on the wars of Louis XI and Charles the Bold, just as he admired the *History of Italy* by Francesco Guicciardini, one of the historical masterpieces of the Renaissance. His interests extended from local history to world history, from Bouchet's *Annals of Aquitaine* to the *History of the Great Kingdom of China* by González de Mendoza.

Montaigne believed that the study of history was an essential ingredient in the education of children (he was thinking of noble boys), because reading history allows one to frequent the company of 'the worthiest minds, who lived in the best ages' (1.26). By the 'best ages' he meant ancient Greece and Rome, as his examples show. Cato the younger was 'a model chosen by nature to show how far human virtue and constancy can reach' (1.37). The essay on 'three good women' is concerned with three Roman matrons, and followed by one on the 'most excellent men' who have ever existed – Homer, Alexander the Great, and the Theban general Epaminondas (2.35, 2.36). The point of this reading is to learn virtue, not to learn dates. A good teacher will 'imprint in his pupils's minds not so much the date of the ruin of Carthage, as the morals of Hannibal and Scipio' (1.26). In suggesting that history taught virtue through the careers of exemplary individuals, Montaigne was very much a man of his time. His cultural relativism was overcome by his admiration for classical antiquity. Only the late essay on coaches suggests that the courage and constancy shown by the Mexicans and Peruvians in their resistance to the Spaniards was equal to 'the most famous ancient examples' (3.6).

The choice of Alexander, Cato and Scipio as heroes was also

conventional enough in Montaigne's day. More unusual was his placing of Homer and Socrates in the same class as the political leaders (above, p.37). So was the suggestion – anodyne as it may seem today – that the main reason for reading history books was that in them could be found the general knowledge of man, 'the variety and truth of his inner conditions, more lively and complete than anywhere else' (2.10). In other words, Montaigne was suggesting that history taught not only virtue but also psychology, revealing, for example, 'how we weep and laugh at the same thing', for Duke René of Lorraine wept for the death of his enemy Charles the Bold (1.38). Although he found the author's comments too cynical, Montaigne was delighted by Guicciardini's *History of Italy* because it was full of maxims about human nature and motivation.

History taught psychology because human nature was, despite the diversity of customs and the difference between one individual and another, essentially the same. This was the justification of Montaigne's study of himself: 'each man bears the whole form of the human condition', form in its Aristotelian sense of pattern, of potential (3.2). 'It is one and the same nature rolling by (*qui roule son cours*). Anyone who has judged the present accurately may draw valid conclusions about the future and the past' (2.12).

At the same time, Montaigne was aware of change, almost to the point of obsession. It was appropriate that his favourite childhood reading should have been Ovid's *Metamorphoses*, for change, together with other forms of diversity, is a central theme of his essays. What an extraordinary variety of terms he uses to describe it: Among the adjectives, *caduque, coulant, roulant, labile, mobile, fluant, remuant, vagabonde, ondoyant*. Among the nouns, *alteration, agitation, branle* ('dance'), *corruption, decadence, declinaison, decrepitude, fluxion, inclination, instabilité, mouvement, mutation, passage, remuement, revolution* (but not in the political sense), *variation*, and *vicissitude*. In this dance of words it may be useful to attempt to pick out some of the different movements, and to formulate distinctions which are implicit in Montaigne, though never formally expressed.

To begin with the author himself, and what he calls his own

'instability'. 'What pleases me now, will soon be painful ... my judgement floats, it wanders' (2.12). This sounds like an apologetic description of an individual quirk of personality, but other passages show that Montaigne was making a point about the human condition. It is always difficult to follow 'a path as wandering as that of the mind'. The self will not remain still for its portrait. Whenever one focuses on it, it dissolves. Hence what is needed is a moving picture, a story. 'I am not describing the essence but the passage ... from day to day, from minute to minute' (3.2).

It is not only the individual who changes. Societies do the same. 'Instability is the worst thing I find in our state; our laws can no more take a stable form than our clothes' (2.17). Ideas change too: sometimes one opinion flourishes, sometimes another. 'The beliefs, judgements and opinions of men ... have their revolutions, their seasons, their births and deaths, like cabbages' (2.12). Morality changes. Montaigne thought that the men of his day were less honest than they used to be, full of simulation and dissimulation. 'Our morals are extremely corrupt, with an extraordinary tendency towards deterioration' (2.17). Montaigne often returned to the theme of the corruption of his own age, as revealed, for example, in the civil wars. However, he made it clear that he believed the trend to be purely local. 'It is absurd of us today to argue the decline and decrepitude of the world from the evidence of our own weakness and decadence.' This is mere ethnocentrism, belied by the discovery of the New World, which is still young at a time when we are old (3.6). Montaigne took the adjectives 'old' and 'young' literally, not metaphorically. 'The infirmities and other conditions of our bodies are also seen in states and governments: kingdoms and commonwealths, like us, are born, flourish and fade with age' (2.23).

From his Olympian viewpoint it was clear to Montaigne that the corruption of manners in France, like his own old age, was no more than a tiny part of the universal flux. 'All things are in continual movement, change and variation' (2.12). 'The world is in perpetual motion (*le monde n'est qu'une branloire perenne*). Everything in it moves incessantly: the earth, the rocks of the

Caucasus, the pyramids of Egypt . . . Constancy itself is nothing but a dance in slower time (*un branle plus languissant*)' (3.2). Some changes can be resisted, at least for a time. Individuals form habits and societies from customs. The laws, he once remarked, 'like our rivers, grow larger and grander as they go (*grossissent et s'ennoblissent en roulant*)' (2.12). He also saw them as a rock of relative stability amid the universal flux, not to be improved by fallible human reason. However, most changes are as sadly inevitable as old age.

How unusual was Montaigne's sense of change? The idea of universal mutability was a classical commonplace. The Greek philosopher Heraclitus, who flourished about 500 BC, argued, as Montaigne himself reminds us, that 'no man ever stepped twice into the same river'. The stoics stressed the inconstancy of worldly affairs, to which the ideal man would respond by his inner constancy, and Seneca in particular expressed an acute sense of the passing of time. It was Seneca too who drew the analogy, later commonplace, between changes in the human body, from infancy to old age, and changes in the 'body politic', the state. Other classical writers, such as Sallust and Juvenal, had a good deal to say about the corruption of morals, the change from primitive simplicity to decadent luxury. All these points were frequently reiterated in the sixteenth century. Many Frenchmen agreed with Montaigne that they lived in an age of decline, though some would have added, unlike him, that this was the old age of the whole world.

Some of Montaigne's contemporaries showed particular sensitivity to particular kinds of change. Protestants were aware of changes in the Church, more especially the gradual decline from 'primitive' poverty and simplicity into wealth and corruption, a decline which they believed it possible to reverse. A group of French lawyers were particularly interested in changes in laws and customs. At the Renaissance there had been a movement to study ancient Roman law in order to revive it, but the more they studied Roman law, the more this group of men became aware that Roman law was not appropriate to their own society because times had changed. In this sense they were relativists. 'The diversity of laws is due to the diversity of manners which arises in people according to the diversity of regions and environment', wrote one of the group, Montaigne's friend Etienne Pasquier. In his *Method for the Easy Understanding of History* (1566), Jean Bodin, another member of this group, declared 'the absurdity of attempting to establish principles of universal jurisprudence from the Roman decrees, which were subject to change within a brief period'. He recommended the study of world history in a systematically comparative way in order to explain 'the beginnings, growth, conditions, change and decline of all states'. Widening out still further, the classical scholar Louis Le Roy devoted a whole treatise to the problem of change, his *Vicissitude, or Variety of Things in the Universe* (1575), a book which dealt with languages and the arts as well as with laws and empires, and with other cultures, including the Arabs, as well as the Greeks and Romans. Le Roy's basic conceptual scheme was that of the cycle of change from roughness to polish and from polish to corruption.

In Le Roy's interpretation of history, the rise and fall of arms and letters, empires and civilisations usually occurred simultaneously. Pasquier, on the other hand, believed that 'commonwealths rise by arms and decline with letters', a view which seems to have been shared by Montaigne. 'Writing seems to be a symptom of an unbalanced age. When did we ever write so much as we have done since our troubles? Or the Romans, as in the time of their decline?' (3.9). Le Roy saw a providential pattern in the 'vicissitudes' of history; in that sense he believed in progress, a spiral rather than a cycle. Bodin, for his part, saw numerological patterns in world history, which he thought influenced by the stars. Montaigne was more modest and more sceptical. It was enough for him to describe change. He did not presume to offer any explanation.

It should be clear that Montaigne's historical and geographical relativism was not unique to him. It was an attitude shared with a group of scholars, mainly lawyers, of more or less his generation, a group to which he belonged by training, early career and personal acquaintance. His reflections on the history of law, language and other institutions were based on less learning than those of Pasquier and possibly some other scholars. His ideas were not developed into a fully-fledged theory like those of Bodin and Le Roy.

On the other hand, Montaigne's vision was broader than theirs, and perhaps deeper as well. He combined the relatively precise sense of institutional change characteristic of the lawyer-antiquarians with the more general sense of flux expressed by philosophers such as Seneca and poets such as Ronsard, and, a little later, by the Italian Marino, the Spaniard Quevedo, and a number of minor French writers. Unlike the stoic and neostoic philosophers, he saw the self, as well as the world, as in flux, and constancy itself as change in slower motion. Of his contemporaries, only the Italian physician Girolamo Cardano (above, p.41) approached him in his sense of the elusiveness of the ever-changing self. Although parallels can be found for virtually every one of the ideas about change to be found in Montaigne, the combination, together with the deep concern with time, is distinctively his own.

This concern with process, with decay, with becoming is reflected as well as expressed in his essays, their apparent inconsistencies and digressions being so many ways to catch the movement of a mind in pursuit of truth. The extent to which Montaigne was a conscious stylist, matching his originality of content with originality of form, will be discussed in the next chapter.

9 Montaigne's aesthetics

Montaigne made no claim to be a literary artist; quite the reverse. He did not want people to discuss the language of the essays, but their content. He declared that he simply wrote down his thoughts as they occurred to him. 'I generally begin without a plan: the first word begets the second' (1.40). ' I speak to the paper, as I speak to the first person I meet' (3.1). He would no doubt have lifted an eyebrow at the suggestion that he had an 'aesthetic', a term which was not used in the sixteenth century. However, he did express forceful and relatively unconventional views about the language of others. In the light of these comments, his own essays look more and more like words of conscious literary art.

'The language I love', Montaigne declared, 'is a simple language, the same for writing as for speaking, rich, vigorous, laconic and pithy (*un parler succulent et nerveux, court et serré*), not delicate and affected, but vehement and brusque ... free, loose and bold (*desreglé, descousu et hardy*) ... not in the style of schoolmasters, or friars, or lawyers, but in that of soldiers (*non pedantesque, non fratesque, non pleideresque, mais plutost soldatesque*)' (1.26).

In other words, Montaigne was against jargon, against strict rules, against magniloquence, and against affectation, such as the 'fantastic Spanish Petrarchist elevations' of some poets of his day, and what he called 'vain subtleties', such as writing poems in the shape of wings or hatchets, as had been done by certain late classical and Renaissance poets – and was to be done again by English 'metaphysical' poets and French 'baroque' ones.

The poetry Montaigne enjoyed was the poetry of his contemporaries Ronsard and Du Bellay, and also what he called 'popular poetry' (*la poësie populaire*), thinking, for example, of the *villanelles* of his native Gascony, or the songs of peoples without writing – he owned transcriptions of some love-songs and war-songs of the Indians of Brazil. As for prose style, he was bold enough to reject Cicero, the model of literary Latin for so many of his contemporaries, as 'boring' (*sa façon d'escrire me semble ennuyeuse*), and to praise the medieval chroniclers Froissart and Commynes for their simplicity, their *franche naïveté* as he calls it. In a similar manner he praised Amyot, the French translator of Plutarch, for the simplicity (*naïveté*) and purity of his language. (The term *naïveté* does not seem to have had the patronising overtones it has since acquired.)

Montaigne's praise of simplicity and of writing as one speaks is not as easy to interpret as it may look. He was opposing rhetorical extravagance but he was not opposing rhetoric. He did not reject all classical models along with Cicero, and still less did he reject literary models altogether. In praising *un parler succulent et nerveux, court et serré*, he was in fact following a literary model and echoing Erasmus's recommendation of a 'weighty, concise and muscular style' (*dicendi genus solidius, astrictius, nervosius*). There was more than one classical model to follow. 'My inclination', Montaigne confessed, 'is to imitate the style of Seneca' (2.17). This was not purely a matter of personal inclination. In the later sixteenth century, Seneca was becoming fashionable as a stylist, just as he was becoming fashionable as a moralist. The so-called 'Senecan amble', the relatively loose and informal construction of his sentences, appealed to Muret, Lipsius and others besides Montaigne. It is true that Seneca does not write like Froissart, but in a more mannered style. However, what was important for Montaigne was what the style of these two writers had in common. They did not write complex sentences with many subordinate clauses in the manner of Cicero, but strung their points together with 'ands' rather than 'therefores', and gave an impression of greater informality.

Informality was appropriate for what Montaigne was trying to do. Since he was more concerned with Brutus at home than with Brutus on the battlefield, it was right for his prose to put off dress uniform for something unbuttoned (*descousu*, one of Montaigne's adjectives for his own style, literally means 'unstitched'). He rejected elaborate rhetoric as he rejected elaborate ceremony. He described his own style on one occasion as 'comic and domestic' (*un stile comique et privé*). By 'comic' he did not mean that he was trying to make the reader laugh; the word had a technical meaning. Classical dramatists wrote in a 'high' or artificial style in their tragedies, devoted to the public lives of the great, but in a 'low' or ordinary style (*sermo humilis*), in their comedies, which were concerned with the private lives of ordinary people. Montaigne was following classical standards of appropriateness ('decorum') by writing in a conversational tone about 'an ordinary life, without distinction', as he described his own.

In any case, the low style had considerable advantages for what Montaigne was trying to do. The loose sentence construction was appropriate for his method of juxtaposing ideas and deliberately suspending judgement. The low style had a word for everything, whereas the high style had a much more restricted vocabulary. One of Montaigne's criticisms of ancient and modern historians was that they left out relevant material because they thought it undignified and because they were unable to express it in the high style (*pour ne la scavoir dire en bon Latin ou François*). Froissart and Commynes scored because they did not aim so high.

Another advantage of the low style is that a well-placed colloquialism is an appropriate instrument for one of Montaigne's favourite literary activities, deflating human pretensions. It brings the reader down to earth with a bump. Man may think he lives in the centre of the universe, but earth is merely 'the ground floor of the house' (*dernier estage du logis*). Empires grow and decay 'like cabbages' (*comme des choux*). Montaigne is of course prepared to turn this weapon on himself. His literary efforts are his 'scribblings', his 'bundle' (*fagotage*), or his 'stew' (*fricassée*). But a term like 'stew' should not be taken to mean that Montaigne had no interest in the cooking.

This is not to suggest that he sat down in his tower one day with the idea of writing 'essays'. Since a number of early essays are not much more than a patchwork or mosaic of quotations from Seneca and other writers, it looks as if they grew out of the common sixteenth-century practice of keeping a 'commonplace book' of memorable sayings and useful pieces of information. It would not be the only book which was created in this fashion.

Erasmus published a collection of classical adages together with his comments on them, and the comments grew longer from edition to edition, so that his remarks on a three-word Latin proverb, *Dulce bellum inexpertis* ('Sweet is war to those who have not experienced it'), ended up as what we would call an 'essay' in praise of peace. In a similar way Montaigne gave less and less attention to the quotations he had assembled, and more and more to his own reactions and reflections.

The idea of publishing a discursive treatment of a number of different subjects within the covers of a single volume was not new in Montaigne's day. For example, in the late fifteenth century the Italian humanist-poet Angelo Poliziano had published his 'Miscellanies'. A common name for this genre was 'discourses', as in the case of Machiavelli's *Discorsi* on, or more exactly around, the first ten books of Livy's history of Rome, or the *Discours politiques et militaires* published in 1587 by the Huguenot gentleman and military leader François de la Noue. In their Italian translation of 1590, Montaigne's essays were entitled 'Moral, Political and Military Discourses'. The genre of discourses was a revival of the Greek *diatribe*, which may be defined as a short treatment of a moral theme, written in a vivid immediate and humorous way, so that the reader has the sense of listening to the author. Plutarch's *Moralia*, one of Montaigne's favourite books, was a collection of 'diatribes' in this sense. So was the *Silva* ('wood', another term for 'miscellany') of the Spanish gentleman Pedro Mexia, whose 120 discourses deal with much the same historical and moral topics as Montaigne; with Heraclitus and Democritus, with cruelty, with the continence of Alexander and Scipio, and so on. Mexia's book was translated into French in 1557 and Montaigne knew it.

The form of the essays owes something to other classical literary genres besides the diatribe. It has a good deal in common with the soliloquy, as exemplified by that of the emperor Marcus Aurelius, and also with the open letter. An example Montaigne knew well was that of Seneca's *Letters to Lucilius* (which were, as Bacon remarked, 'dispersed meditations' or essays), and he was also familiar with some sixteenth-century Italian letter collections. Some of his essays were, like letters, addressed to individuals of his acquaintance; *On the education of children* to Diane de Foix, and *On the resemblance of children to their parents*, to Madame de Duras. Another genre which has left its mark on the essays is the paradox, such as the praise of ignorance, which can be found in Plutarch and also in some sixteenth-century writers known to Montaigne, such as Agrippa, Gelli and Landi, not to mention Erasmus's *Praise of Folly*.

Out of the diatribe, the letter, the soliloquy and the paradox Montaigne gradually developed a form of his own, which is most distinctive not in its length or subject-matter but rather in its author's attempt to catch himself in the act of thinking, to present the process of thought, *le progrez de mes humeurs*, rather than the conclusions. This was the point of giving the collection the title, then unusual, of *essais*: 'attempts', 'trials', or even, perhaps, 'experiments'. It is in this sense that Montaigne was the creator of a new literary genre.

The essay in his own individual sense was a shoe of exactly the shape for Montaigne's foot, a genre which would allow him to talk about himself, to question what others took for granted without committing himself one way or the other, and to digress. Digression was a standard rhetorical device, but not on this scale. His book is in some ways remarkably open, frank and immediate, and it speaks to us across the centuries as few sixteenth-century books do.

In other ways, however, the book is extremely opaque, reticent, paradoxical and ambiguous. The labels on certain essays seem to have nothing to do with the contents. 'Custom of the island of Cea' is largely devoted to the problem of suicide; 'On some verses of Virgil', with attitudes to sex; 'On coaches', with the New World; 'On the lame', with witchcraft. It is always possible that the digression ran away with the essay on these occasions, but it is more likely that Montaigne was planning to give the reader a surprise. He may also have been making things difficult for the censor, and making sure that he was not condemned by anyone who did not take the trouble to read more than the chapter headings.

Another paradox is that Montaigne's book is stuffed with quotations (1,264 from the Latin classics, about 800 from proverbs and similar material), yet suggests that generalisations are impossible and even that 'there were never two identical opinions in the world, any more than two hairs, or two grains' (2.37). As unlike as two peas, one might say. It is characteristic of Montaigne to turn a proverb upside down in this way, just as it is characteristic of him to place quotations in such a context that they convey a different meaning from that of the original author. Again, he claims to compose by a kind of free association ('the first word begets the second') whereas his essays do in fact have a formal structure, often that of a circular tour at the end of which we are led to glimpse familiar notions and customs from an unfamiliar angle. As in a symphony, themes recur and apparent digressions and parentheses often suggest conclusions which are never stated openly. At one point he warned the reader to expect this. 'I express my opinions here so far as custom allows me; I point with my finger to what I cannot say openly' (3.9).

Like Socrates, Montaigne seems to have no opinions but is in fact sometimes manipulative. Like Castiglione's ideal courtier, Montaigne put considerable effort into achieving the effect of spontaneity. For a declared enemy of rhetoric as 'vanity of words' he made a remarkably full use of the figures of speech, notably irony. At times he produced brilliant rhetorical set-pieces, notably in the apologia for Sebond, which is at once an oration on the misery of man (an anti-Pico), and a philippic against the uncertainty and vanity of learning, in the manner of the 'declamation' on the same subject written earlier in the century by the German humanist Agrippa von Nettesheim.

It is hard to resist the conclusion that Montaigne's critique of rhetoric functions, at least on occasion, as a form of rhetoric, a technique of persuasion. It lessens the reader's resistance to disturbing ideas. So does the image of the author as a 'plain man', a persona which is projected too skilfully for Montaigne to have been anything of the kind. The 'I' of the essays – one might call him 'Michel' – is as much a literary device as Proust's 'Marcel'. It is scarcely surprising to find that – as the next chapter will suggest – Montaigne has often been misunderstood.

'I add, but I correct nothing . . . my book is altogether one' (3.9), Montaigne claimed in one of the last essays. He certainly added a good deal. The 1588 edition contained numerous interpolations in books one and two of the *Essays*, as well as a new book three; scholars call this the 'B-text' to distinguish it from the 1580 version. Montaigne annotated his own copy of this 1588 edition (the 'Bordeaux copy', as it is called), and added about a thousand more passages, thus creating a third version, the 'C-text'. But did he really alter nothing? So acutely aware of his changes from minute to minute, as we have seen, Montaigne seems to have been virtually unconscious of his intellectual development from 1572 to 1592, from the time he began writing till his death. In this respect he differs markedly from Rousseau, Goethe, and the many autobiographers who have followed in their wake, writers whose main theme was precisely their intellectual or spiritual development.

If Montaigne was not aware of his own development, what can posterity hope to know about it? We can in fact know something, thanks to the careful detective work of one of the greatest of Montaigne scholars, Pierre Villey – although his conclusions are not accepted by all the specialists. Villey worked out when Montaigne read a number of his favourite books; Caesar in 1578, López de Gómara between 1584 and 1588, Herodotus and Plato after 1588, and so on. Villey also dated the composition of forty-five essays to the period 1572–4, and of forty-nine more to the period 1575–80. For the years 1580–1, there is a record of Montaigne's thoughts in the journal he kept while travelling in Italy and elsewhere. For the period 1580–8, we have the third book of the *Essays* and the B-text of books one and two, and for 1588–92, the after-thoughts of the Bordeaux copy. On this evidence, together with some letters, Villey based his famous study of 'the evolution of Montaigne', published in 1908.

What was this 'evolution'? Villey divided Montaigne's

intellectual life into three. There was the stoic period of his youth; a sceptical period, following a crisis in the middle of the 1570s; and a final mature period in which Montaigne expressed his faith in the essential goodness of man. These three periods correspond more or less with the three books of the *Essays*.

It is always somewhat artificial and misleading to carve people up into periods, as if the young Marx, to take a much-debated example, was not the same person as the author of *Capital*, and as if we were not – as Montaigne saw so clearly – changing all the time. Whatever we think of the three periods, however, it is difficult to disagree with Villey about the general direction of Montaigne's development. The evidence for his early stoicism includes the letter he wrote in 1563, on the death of his friend La Boétie, praising him for his tranquillity of mind and for the 'invincible courage' with which he met death's assaults. The first group of essays are thoroughly impregnated with stoic values. An obvious example is the argument that good and evil largely depend on our attitudes towards them (1.14). The early essays are rather short, and they indulge their author's taste for moral maxims. It is in these essays that Montaigne is most typical of his age.

Then came what Villey calls Montaigne's 'sceptical crisis', when he was in his early forties. The change can be dated to 1575–6 because Montaigne had his 'que sais-je?' medal struck at this time, when he was writing his apologia for Sebond. Whether 'crisis' is the best description of Montaigne's change of mind is less clear. It is a strong term, implying psychological shock as well as a clean break with the past. It can obviously be a shock to find oneself doubting what one had previously taken for granted, but we have no concrete evidence of Montaigne's emotional reactions at this time, and in any case the author of the apologia for Sebond does not give the impression of a man in a state of shock. On the contrary, he is very much in control of his argument.

As for the essays in the third book, they are different from the rest in a number of ways, and especially different from the ones composed in the early 1570s. They are much longer; on average, as Villey pointed out, an essay in book three is six times the length of an essay in book one. The later essays rely less on quotations to make their points, but draw on autobiography instead, a sign of the emancipation from intellectual authorities which is recommended in the remarks on the education of children (1.26). The later essays are more critical of the stoics, and much bolder altogether; Montaigne is, for example, more and more outspoken in his opposition to torture. His opinions became less and less like those of other men of his generation. He gained control of the essay form, or rather, he developed it into something which was distinctively his own. In short, one has a much stronger impression from the third book than from the others that Montaigne had found both what he wanted to say and how to say it.

To say that Montaigne had found himself at last implies that he had changed, but also implies a fundamental constancy; not so much a case of 'evolution' (Villey's rather dated term) as 'development' in its original sense of unfolding, unrolling, in other words of revealing what had really been there all the time. It has to be added that on certain questions Montaigne did change his mind altogether. He had once been rather contemptuous of ordinary people, 'the vulgar', as the upper classes generally were, but he came to have a more positive attitude towards them, to attribute to them some of the virtues he admired in the savages of Brazil. He came to place private values above public ones, to admire Alexander the Great less and Socrates more. He had once believed, with the stoics, that philosophy taught us how to die. He ended by thinking that what it taught was how to live (3.2). In his late forties, Montaigne came to accept himself as never before. He concluded that it is 'an absolute perfection, and virtually divine, to know how truly to enjoy one's own nature' (*scavoyr jouyr loiallement de son estre*) (3.13). He had achieved that serenity which he once defined as the distinguishing mark of wisdom.

If we can rely on Montaigne's own account of his former beliefs, referring (presumably) to the period before 1572, then another important change comes into view. He had 'once', so he tells us, 'taken the liberty of making my own choice and of ignoring certain points in the practice of our Church which seemed somewhat misguided or odd (*qui semblent avoir un visage ou plus vain ou plus estrange*). Once, he continues, 'if I heard someone talking of ghosts, or prophecies, magic or sorcery ... I would feel pity for the poor people who were taken in by these follies.' Now, he was no longer so confident (1.27). Scepticism cuts both ways; to suspend judgement is as different from disbelieving in witches as from believing in them. In other words – modern words – he believed that he had gone beyond rationalism.

Montaigne once criticised biographers who made their subjects too consistent, 'arranging and interpreting all the actions of a certain person' according to their fixed idea or image of that person, and so doing violence to reality (2.1). This would be a fatal mistake to make in Montaigne's own case. He was not a systematic thinker, but a man full of insights, some of which are not consistent with others. His attitudes in later life are most easy to understand as the product of a process of development in which he reacted against some of his earlier views (as in the examples quoted above), without always quite giving them up.

His contemporaries, however, either failed to notice the new Montaigne, or found it necessary to excuse the change they saw. Montaigne was much admired and much read in his own day, and the *Essays* went through five editions between 1580 and 1588. But generally speaking, the Montaigne who was most appreciated and imitated was the early Montaigne, stoic and sententious, the Montaigne who most resembled his contemporaries. His friend Florimond de Raemond, writing in 1594, noted his 'courageous and almost stoic philosophy' (*sa philosophie courageuse et presque stoïque*). Another contemporary, Claude Expilly, called him a 'great-minded stoic'. Pasquier, another friend of Montaigne's, saw the *Essays* as a 'seedbed of beautiful and memorable maxims'. He did not much care for the third book. His verdict was that Montaigne was a bold man who allowed himself to be carried away by his wit and chose to mock the reader, and perhaps himself as well. In other words, a good deal of what we tend to find most interesting in Montaigne went unnoticed by his contemporaries or was dismissed as nothing but amiable eccentricity.

Even the term 'essay' had a warmer welcome on this side of the Channel, where it was taken up by Francis Bacon (1597) and Sir William Cornwallis (1600). However, in France in the late sixteenth century the 'discourse' form was popular and this popularity probably owes something to Montaigne's example. There were the *Serées* of Guillaume Bouchet (1584), which, like Montaigne, discuss impotence and torture; the *Matinées* of Nicholas Cholières (1585); and the *Bigarrures* of Etienne Tabourot (1584), who declared, in the manner of Montaigne, that he 'observed no order, but heaped up examples pell-mell as they came to mind', and went so far in imitation as to write discourses on the education of children and on pseudo-witches.

Pierre Charron (1541–1603), a priest who knew Montaigne well and was a house guest in his château, was even more of a disciple. His treatise on wisdom (1601), with its separate chapters on human vanity, misery, inconstancy, presumption, and so on, expresses the sceptical-fideist view of the world of Montaigne's apologia for Sebond in more systematic – and more dogmatic – form. The difference between them is expressed in the mottoes of the two men. Where Montaigne chose *Que sais-je?*, Charron preferred *Je ne sais*.

In the first two-thirds of the seventeenth century, Montaigne was still much appreciated in France. The *Essays* continued to be reprinted every two or three years; at least five times in 1608, six times in 1617, five times in 1627, nine times in 1636. The bishop of Belley, Jean-Pierre Camus (1584–1654), was, like Charron, a Counter-Reformation cleric who found fideism attractive. His *Diversités* – yet another synonym for 'essays' – drew heavily on Plutarch, Seneca and Montaigne, whose essays he called 'the gentleman's breviary'. The philosopher Pierre Gassendi (1592–1655), another priest, was an admirer of Montaigne and Charron and a declared disciple of Sextus Empiricus. Some of Gassendi's friends shared his enthusiasm, notably François La Mothe Le Vayer (1588–1672), who wrote dialogues on scepticism, and Cardinal Richelieu's librarian, Gabriel Naudé (1600–53). Gassendi, La Mothe and Naudé all had the reputation of *libertins*, a fashionable pejorative term of the seventeenth century with associations of atheism, cynicism, hedonism and sexual immorality. Cyrano de Bergerac (1619–55), another admirer of Montaigne, best known for his account of a voyage to the moon, was tarred with the same brush. How far this group went in their unorthodoxy it is difficult to say. Perhaps they were Catholics, despite their mockery of popular devotion. Perhaps they were deists, whose God was remote and impersonal, without interest in the world of men. Perhaps they were materialists who denied providence and believed the universe to be the result of chance, in the manner of Epicurus and Lucretius, authors they certainly admired.

What the group saw in Montaigne is somewhat easier to determine. His rejection of intellectual authorities appealed to them. Cyrano and La Mothe were attracted by his cultural relativism, while Naudé praised him for his style and his 'great abundance of maxims' and criticised credulous witch-hunters in a similar vein, while preferring the more methodical Charron. Naudé was too much the rationalist and too much the Aristotelian to accept Montaigne altogether. His motto was 'to square everything by the level of reason' (*esquarrer toutes choses au niveau de la raison*). The group incorporated important elements of Montaigne's thought into their own intellectual systems, inevitably giving these elements a somewhat different significance from their original one.

Montaigne was also well known outside France in the seventeenth century. In England, for example, Bacon's *Essays* owe something to the example of Montaigne, though his taut sentences and crisp generalisations are the antithesis of Montaigne in the sense that they seem designed to end a discussion rather than to provoke one. Florio's somewhat free translation of Montaigne goes back to 1603. It is likely that Shakespeare read him in this version, and that *The Tempest* owes something to the essay on cannibals. Sir Thomas Browne was another admirer of Montaigne and indeed a kindred spirit – essayist, fideist and explorer of himself. So was Joseph Glanvill, whose *Vanity of Dogmatising* (1661), dealt with a theme close to Montaigne's heart.

However, in the later seventeenth century there was a reaction against Montaigne. Descartes had something to do with it. In a sense Descartes was a sceptic in the tradition of Montaigne, for he began by doubting everything, but he ended very differently, with his picture of the universe as a vast machine. Montaigne regarded animals as intelligent in the same way that men are intelligent; Descartes thought of them as clockwork. Montaigne had helped undermine the traditional view of the hierarchical universe, but did not put anything systematic in its place. Those who accepted the new mechanical world picture inevitably saw Montaigne as old-fashioned.

The devout also turned against him. Montaigne had sometimes been attacked as an 'atheist' in his own day, but this seems to have been a minority view until the 1660s, when the leading churchman Bishop Bossuet preached against him. Blaise Pascal (1623–62) criticised Montaigne in his posthumously published *Pensées* for the 'foolish plan' of portraying himself, and also for his 'quite pagan attitudes to death'. He studied Montaigne carefully, taking over a number of his ideas and even phrases, but only to incorporate them into a very different moral and theological structure of his own. Nicolas Malebranche, Cartesian philosopher and Catholic theologian, was against Montaigne on both counts. The *Essays* were placed on the Roman Index in 1676 (the Spaniards, with their keener noses for heresy, had placed him on their Index in 1640). It has been argued with some plausibility that the reaction against Montaigne had much to do with the changing position of the Catholic Church. In the 1580s, the main threat to the Church came from the Protestants. Montaigne was clearly no Protestant; indeed, his scepticism could be used as a weapon against Protestants, to sap their confidence in private judgement. By the later seventeenth century, however, the sceptic or 'libertine' seemed the chief threat to the Church, and so Montaigne's own unorthodoxy seemed more questionable. It should be added that the admiration which Naudé and his circle felt for Montaigne can have done him no good with the devout. It is a difficult question to decide whether the seventeenth-century censors, who put Montaigne on the Index, were more perceptive than their sixteenth-century colleagues, or whether they simply associated him with seventeenth-century misunderstandings of his work. His cultural relativism, which had so attracted Cyrano de Bergerac, was now forgotten. Bossuet's *Discourse on World History* (1681) is simply a history of western (classical-Jewish-Christian) civilisation, written as if China (and Montaigne) had never existed. Perhaps this collective amnesia was necessary for the intellectual stability of the age of Louis XIV. Only the Protestant sceptic Pierre Bayle (1647–1706) carried on the Montaigne tradition. His *Various Thoughts on the Comet* (1683) is a critique of human ethnocentrism in the same class as the apologia for Raymond Sebond.

There were also aesthetic reasons for the slump in Montaigne's reputation in the later seventeenth century. In the age of classicism, the loose construction of his essays was no longer pleasing. One leading French writer, Guez de Balzac (1597–1654), criticised Montaigne because his arguments were broken up by digressions (*son discours ... est un corps en pièces*). Another writer, Charles Sorel (1602–74) complained that the essays 'lacked order and connection'. Pascal condemned what he called Montaigne's 'confusion'. These criticisms, religious and aesthetic, were effective; no French editions of Montaigne were published between 1669 and 1724, though a new English translation, more faithful than Florio's, was produced by Charles Cotton in 1685.

In the eighteenth century, Montaigne was rediscovered – and also reinterpreted. The 1724 edition, the first for more than fifty years, was published in London by a Frenchman who had translated Locke and thought of Montaigne primarily as Locke's precursor, particularly in his ideas on the education of children. The informal style came back into fashion at this time as part of the reaction against the values associated with Louis XIV. Denis Diderot (1713–84) appreciated Montaigne for the very disorder Pascal had condemned, seeing it as spontaneity. It is true that by the eighteenth century the language of Montaigne was beginning to seem quaint and even difficult, but it could always be modernised, and in some editions it was. The ideas were brought up to date as well as the prose. Readers of David Hume's *Essay on Miracles* (1748) almost inevitably interpreted Montaigne's remarks on miracles in a similar way. Was this to 'unfold' his meaning or to obscure it? Voltaire, who fought his own battles against western ethnocentrism and appreciated Montaigne as an ally, once compared him to Montesquieu, a much more systematic thinker. Diderot compared him to the eighteenth-century philosopher Helvétius. In short, Montaigne was seen as a *philosophe*. After 1789, we even find Montaigne the revolutionary. A certain Rabaut de Saint Etienne declared that when Montaigne doubted and Bacon experimented, 'they were preparing the French Revolution'.

Since the Enlightenment there have been several more Montaignes. For the German writer J.G. Herder (1744–1803), he stood for the appreciation of folksong and the return to nature. For the essayist William Hazlitt he was 'the first who had the courage to say as an author what he felt as a man'. Nietzsche admired him for his cultural relativism and his 'brave and cheerful scepticism', and tried to go beyond him in the same direction. Pierre Villey saw him as one who took ' a first step' in the direction of Bacon and a science based on empirical facts (in other words, the positivism of Auguste Comte). E.M. Forster, on the other hand, who once declared that 'My law-givers are Erasmus and Montaigne, not Moses and St Paul' saw him as representing the values of tolerance and loyalty to one's friends rather than to one's country.

We of the later twentieth century cannot afford to scoff at these past images, for we too have created a Montaigne of our own, or rather several. Claude Lévi-Strauss paid homage to Montaigne the ethnologist by calling one of his books *La Pensée sauvage*, a reference to the essay on cannibals. For R.A. Sayce, one of the most perceptive of the recent students of Montaigne, he is 'the first of the great modern bourgeois writers', who comes 'very close to Proust' in his analysis of feelings. Montaigne's disappointment on reaching Venice and finding it less marvellous than he expected is not at all unlike that of 'Marcel' at Balbec. Others have stressed Montaigne's anticipations of Freud, and his attitude to school has reminded one commentator of Ivan Illich. His stoic slogan 'follow Nature' is bound to acquire a new resonance in the next few years, and it can only be a matter of time before he is interpreted as a Taoist. Indeed, he does resemble the Taoists in his relativism, his trust in nature, his acceptance of death, just as the simple life lived by the Greek philosopher Diogenes, whom Montaigne often cites with approval, resembles that of the Taoist Hsü Yü, down to the detail of throwing away the unnecessary drinking vessel.

Such a variety of judgements would have amused Montaigne and ought to worry us. How can a book change its meaning for each successive generation? When we look at Montaigne's self-portrait, do we really see no more than our own reflection in the glass? This is of course a general problem. All the classics are reinterpreted afresh by every generation; if this does not happen, they cease to be classics.

However, it is the function of intellectual historians to warn their own generation of the distortions involved in this reinterpretation of the past, in treating Montaigne (like Shakespeare, or Dante) as our contemporary. We need to remember that he is not one of us, that his fideism, for example, or his use of classical antiquity as a point of reference, sets him apart from us. It is somewhat ethnocentric, not to say patronising, to treat Montaigne as an honorary member of the twentieth century. We would do better to ask ourselves how he would criticise society were he alive today.

And yet most of the interpretations of Montaigne which I have mentioned – perhaps all of them – do contain a kernel of truth. To see him as a *philosophe*, a psychologist or an ethnologist is to direct attention to ideas which he put forward and which some readers have neglected, even if it gives these ideas a disproportionate importance and locates them in a new context. There is a sense in which we are right to talk of the post-humous development of the *Essays*, of latent meanings gradually becoming manifest, of truth as the daughter of time. Some writers, thinkers, and artists seem to be particularly myriad-minded, multi-faceted, or 'polyvalent', and so they continue to appeal to a succession of very different posterities. Perhaps this is the secret of a 'past master'. In any case, there can be little doubt, after four hundred years, that Montaigne is, like Thomas

More, like Shakespeare, like Socrates, like Michelangelo, a man for all seasons. Despite the hundreds of imitations which the *Essays* have inspired, it remains what its author once called it, 'the only book in the world of its kind'.

Further reading

The Pléiade edition of Montaigne (Paris, 1962) includes the letters and travel journal and has the advantage of making clear which portions of the *Essays* belong to the A-, B- and C-texts. A good modern translation is that by D.M. Frame (New York, 1957). John Florio's lively translation of 1603 has often been reprinted.

Among the best general studies of the man and the book are P. Villey, *Les Sources et l'évolution des essais de Montaigne* (2 vols, Paris, 1908); H. Friedrich, *Montaigne* (Bern, 1949, in German; French trans., Paris, 1968); D.M. Frame, *Montaigne: a biography* (London, 1965); R.A. Sayce, *The Essays of Montaigne* (London, 1972).

1 *Montaigne in his time*

On Montaigne's social group, G. Huppert, *Les Bourgeois Gentilshommes* (Chicago and London, 1977 – in English); on his generation, W.L. Gundersheimer, 'The Crisis of the late French Renaissance', in *Renaissance Studies in Honor of Hans Baron*, ed. A. Molho and J. Tedeschi (Florence, 1971). On the ideal of rural retirement – despite its focus on eighteenth-century England – M. Mack, *The Garden and the City* (London, 1969).

2 *Montaigne's humanism*

On humanism in general, P.O. Kristeller, *Renaissance Thought* (New York, 1961); C. Trinkaus, *In Our Image and Likeness* (2 vols, London, 1970), especially part 2, and *Humanism in France*, ed. A.H.T. Levi (Manchester, 1970). On Montaigne, Friedrich, chs 2–4; R. Trinquet, *La Jeunesse de Montaigne* (Paris, 1972), chs 12–14; D.M. Frame, *Montaigne's Discovery of Man* (New York, 1955). For samples of Montaigne's favourite classical authors, Plutarch, *Moral Essays* (trans. R. Warner, Harmondsworth, 1971), and Seneca, *Letters from a Stoic* (trans. R. Campbell, Harmondsworth, 1969).

3 *Montaigne's scepticism*

On the history of the movement, G. Leff, *Medieval Thought* (Harmondsworth, 1958), part 3; R.H. Popkin, *The History of Scepticism from Erasmus to Descartes* (second ed., Assen, 1964); C. Schmitt, *Cicero Scepticus: a Study of the Influence of the Academica in the Renaissance* (The Hague, 1972). For the key texts, Sextus Empiricus, *Outlines of Pyrrhonism* (trans. R.G. Bury, London, 1933), and Cicero, *Academica* (trans. H. Rackham, London, 1933). On Montaigne in particular, besides Popkin, ch. 3, C.B. Brush, *Montaigne and Bayle* (The Hague, 1966); Z. Gierczynski, 'Le Scepticisme de Montaigne', *Kwartalnik Neofilologiczny*, 1967; E. Limbrick, 'Was Montaigne really a Pyrrhonian?', *Bibliothèque d'Humanisme et Renaissance*, 39, 1977.

4 *Montaigne's religion*

H. J. J. Janssen, *Montaigne fidéiste* (Nijmegen and Utrecht, 1930); M. Dréano, *La Pensée religieuse de Montaigne* (Paris, 1936, new ed. 1969). On the Counter-Reformation, P. Spriet, 'Montaigne, Charron et la crise morale', *French Review*, 1965; on miracles, J. Céard, *La Nature et les Prodiges* (Geneva, 1977); on witches, A. Boase, 'Montaigne et les sorcières', in *Culture et politique en France à l'époque de l'humanisme*, ed. F. Simone (Turin, 1974).

5 *Montaigne's politics*

On the background, J. E. Neale, *The Age of Catherine de'Medici* (London, 1943): N.Z. Davis, *Society and Culture in Early Modern France* (London, 1975); Q. Skinner, *Foundations of Modern Political Thought* (Cambridge, 1979), especially vol. 2. R.N. Carew Hunt, 'Montaigne and the State', *Edinburgh Review*, 1927; E. Williamson, 'On the liberalizing of Montaigne', *French Review*, 1949; F.S. Brown, *Religious and Political Conservatism in the Essais of Montaigne* (Geneva, 1963). Extracts from the thesis of J.P. Dhommeaux, 'Les idées politiques de Montaigne', are printed in the *Bulletin de la Société des Amis de Montaigne*, 1976.

6 *Montaigne as psychologist*

On the history of self-portrayal, G. Misch, *Geschichte der Autobiographie*, especially vol. 4 (Frankfurt, 1969), part 2.

On Montaigne, Friedrich, ch. 5; J. Chateau, *Montaigne psychologue* (Paris, 1966); L. R. Entin-Bates, 'Montaigne's remarks on impotence', *Modern Language Notes*, 1976; D. Coleman, 'Montaigne's "sur des vers de Virgile"' in *Classical Influences on European Culture, 1500–1700*, ed. R.R. Bolgar (Cambridge, 1976).

7 *Montaigne as ethnographer*

G. Chinard, *L'Exotisme américain dans la littérature française au 16e siècle* (Paris, 1911); M.T. Hodgen, *Early Anthropology in the Sixteenth and Seventeenth Centuries* (Philadelphia, 1964); D.F. Lach, *Asia in the Making of Europe*, 2 (Chicago, 1977), especially book 2, pp. 286–301; G. Gliozzi, *Adamo e il nuovo mondo* (Florence, 1977), pp. 199–219.

8 *Montaigne as historian*

On the background, D.R. Kelley, *Foundations of Modern Historical Scholarship* (New York, 1970); G. Huppert, *The Idea of Perfect History* (Urbana, 1970); R.J. Quinones, *The Renaissance Discovery of Time* (Cambridge, Mass., 1972).

On Montaigne, G. Poulet, *Etudes sur le temps humain* (Paris, 1950), ch. 1; F. Joukovsky, *Montaigne et le problème du temps* (Paris, 1972); O. Naudeau, *La Pensée de Montaigne* (Geneva, 1972), ch. 3.

9 *Montaigne's aesthetics*

M. Croll, *Style, rhetoric and rhythm* (Princeton, 1966), collects his essays of the 1920s on the anti-ciceronian movement. Friedrich, ch. 8, a general study. On the prehistory of the essay, P.M. Schon, *Vorformen des Essays in Antike und Humanismus* (Wiesbaden, 1954). On Montaigne and the baroque, I. Buffum, *Studies in the Baroque* (New Haven, 1957, ch. 1. On Montaigne's rhetoric, M. McGowan, *Montaigne's Deceits* (London, 1974), and M.M. Phillips, 'From the *Ciceronianus* to Montaigne',

Classical Influences on European Culture, 1500–1700, ed. R.R. Bolgar (Cambridge, 1976).

10   *The development of the* Essays

P. Villey, *Sources et évolution;* P. Villey, *Montaigne devant la postérité* (Paris, 1935); A.M. Boase, *The Fortunes of Montaigne* (London, 1935); D.M. Frame, *Montaigne in France, 1812–1852* (New York, 1940); C. Dédéyan, *Montaigne dans le romantisme anglo-saxon* (Paris, 1944); M. Dréano, *La Renommée de Montaigne, 1677–1802* (Angers, 1952).

Index